OUT OF ORDER

Faith is Strengthened, Hope Blossoms, and Love Conquers After Loss!

By
Judith Orlando Shirilla

DEDICATION

To my two loving children,

Nicholas S. Shirilla

And

Lindsey N. Shirilla

And to my late husband,

Nick E. Shirilla

ISBN 0-936369-41-8

143 Greenfield Road
New Wilmington, PA 16142
1-800-358-0777

Printed in the U.S.A.

ACKNOWLEDGEMENTS

- In memory of my late loving husband, Nick, who fought an eight-year battle with a brain tumor.

- To all those special individuals, who have lost their life in the battle with cancer, but have touched and changed my life in the process.

- For my two loving and courageous children.

- Special thanks to clergy, friends and Nick's co-workers and company for all their support through our ordeal.

- Special thanks to Heidi Walski for using her artistic attributes for my cover design.

- For the dedicated doctors, surgeons, nurses and hospital staff who cared for Nick untiringly.

- For the wonderful treatments Nick underwent.

- For the wonderful poems, verses, books and reference material I used in writing my book.

- For the cancer survivors – their courage is a blessing.

- For Melva Libb, for her editing skills and her help in putting this book together.

- Last but not least, for my faith in God.

INTRODUCTION

Hi. My name is Judith Shirilla. My friends and family call me Judy – so can you. My story is one of profound love, heartache, and dealing with terminal illness; one of encouragement, hope and determination. In the past 13 years I have encountered many obstacles I never could have imagined were possible.

My knowledge of the Christian faith has brought me to a point in my life where I know that no matter what obstacles I encounter, no matter what trials or hardships are handed to me, I can deal with them. I can survive and conquer. I have learned that with God all things are possible.

Please join me as I recount the happenings of the recent years when I experienced a nearly perfect life become transformed into disruption, disappointment and heartbreaking changes.

My story begins like this...

I.
INITIAL DIAGNOSIS
(May 16, 1987)

Life in Order

I looked at my husband. "Nick, do you like the house?"
"Yeah, do you?

"I love it! Let's buy this one." Just moments before we made our decision, a realtor had unlocked a front door and my husband and I had stepped into a vacant home in suburban Boardman, Ohio. "Someone really has taken care of this place," I thought to myself as my feet touched the square of plastic that protected a brand new plush living room carpet.

I loved the kitchen, warm and cozy, decorated in Williamsburg rust and blue with pretty heart borders around the windows. "Wow! It feels like home!" I told Nick.

Before we even toured the small bath and 3 spacious bedrooms I had fallen in love with this ranch home - not the largest or most prestigious, but with sufficient living space and in excellent move-in condition.

I commented, "There's no family room."

Nick grinned as he eyed my protruding stomach, which held our first child. "You know I can always finish the basement." To our surprise, our tour came to an end in a basement that was already paneled and carpeted.

For over a year and a half we had been shopping for what was to be the ideal dwelling place for our future together, the ideal location to raise a family. Looking around the spacious family room, I concluded, "God has guided us to our first home.

The realtor walked toward the steps as if he was in a hurry to leave. "Okay," he commented in a nonchalant manner. "If you'd like to see this place again. I can show it to you Friday or Saturday.

I turned to Nick. "Since it's in such excellent condition, it'll be sold before this weekend."

He nodded in agreement. So that very night we submitted a bid.

February, 1987. We got the house! What a difference it would make, living in our own home instead of an apartment. How could life be any better?

Twenty-seven years old, I still considered myself a newlywed – a very happy newlywed of 2 ½ years. A registered nurse, I loved my part time job, working 3:00 to 11:00 on a Cardiac Care Unit at a nearby hospital. We cared for patients who were transferred there for five to seven days of rehabilitation 24 to 48 hours after open-heart surgery.

My husband Nick was a year older than I. The machine shop where he worked was not far from the house we had just purchased. The family who owned the shop opened their hearts to everyone who worked there, looking upon each employee as someone who had something unique to contribute to their business. Nick had been employed there for eight years and had never taken a day off because of sickness. He worked Monday through Friday, which left the weekends free.

Six feet tall, 195 pounds, Nick was strong, athletic and handsome. Everyone who knew him loved his sense of humor and his gentle, loving manner. Nick enjoyed watching

Nascar races, working out and playing in an intramural basketball league. We loved to bowl and golf together and set aside every Sunday as the time to be with my family and his.

The month of March was filled with excitement as we prepared to move into our new home and attended Lamaze classes to prepare us for the arrival of our first child.

I felt wonderful during my pregnancy. I was able to continue to work throughout the whole nine months. Nurse's training made me aware of the importance of eating healthy foods and drinking milk. I drank eight glasses a day. Many friends and family members commented, "Judy, there's a glow about you."

I especially loved being pregnant because my migraine headaches stopped. I told my doctor, "I could be pregnant forever. I feel wonderful!"

He laughed. "Nobody can be pregnant forever, Judy."

Besides preparing for the arrival of our first child and the move, Nick was working 12-hour shifts. He also managed to find time to condition our prized one-year-old Buick Regal for spring, removing the snow tires and replacing them with beautiful sports wheels.

His energy seemed to be endless. "What would you like me to pack?" he'd ask when I walked in the door after work.

Nick and I were so excited, wondering if our child would be a boy or a girl.

"It doesn't matter to me, just as long as it's healthy," I would say. I often prayed for my baby to be healthy.

Looking back, I compare the happiness Nick and I shared with the bubbles children love to blow. They come in such interesting shapes and reflect such pretty colors. They are translucent, simple and so much fun.

A happy marriage, a new house, jobs that we loved, an expected baby, a loving family – a fantasy land, an exhilarating merry-go-round ride with happy music playing and the horses gliding round and round. Life was far better than I ever could have expected.

Our Bubbles Burst

My anticipated due date was May 23, 1987. On Saturday evening, May 16, Nick and I went to dinner with Jan, one of my 3 sisters, and her husband Jack. Jack had graduated with my husband from high school. After dinner, we had gone to their house to watch a movie. What a busy day! What fun, spending the evening with Jan and Jack.

Late that night it felt good to crawl into bed to relax and dream of moving day which would be within the week. Nearly all our belongings were packed and ready to go. We planned to move all our belongings into the house, but stay with my parents for a few days so we could repaint the inside of our new house. Everything would be fresh and clean, ready for the arrival of our baby.

I was just falling off to sleep when Nick said, "Judy, I've got a funny feeling in my chest. It's like a burning sensation."

"I'll get you some Mylanta," I told him as I pulled myself up and got out of bed.

The day before, he had mentioned to me that he had been experiencing what he called "dizzy spells" at work. He'd explained, "Sometimes I feel like everything is going in slow motion. Sometimes when we're walking up to the front door of the church, I feel the same way."

Of course, my nurse's training kicked into action. "Do you get a headache? Do you feel like you're going to fall down? Maybe you have an ear infection."

I had called our family doctor. After he had given Nick a complete physical he told me, "I don't seem to find anything except a little fluid in his ear."

"Umm, okay," I had responded. "So maybe it was his inner ear."

As our doctor began to write on his prescription pad, he said to Nick, "I'm going to start you on an antibiotic. If this doesn't clear up, I may have to bring you in for a neurological work-up in a couple of weeks." I had noticed a disturbed expression on my husband's face.

I gave Nick the Mylanta, then recalled that visit to the doctor as I climbed back into bed, surprised that Nick had already fallen asleep. I could not get my mind to slow down. A neurological work-up? I couldn't forget the look on Nick's face.

The baby began to move around, pressing on everything so much that I had to sit up. I reached for my prayer book on the nightstand and prayed some of the prayers that I frequently used throughout my pregnancy.

Suddenly Nick began to thrash violently. I felt hysterical, screaming out, "God, please don't let him die! I don't want to raise this baby all alone!"

God heard my frantic plea. As suddenly as the thrashing had begun, it stopped. My husband lay perfectly still. His teeth were tightly clenched, his mouth as blue as could be.

This was a familiar sight for a nurse. I thought to myself. "He just had a seizure!"

During a grand mal seizure, the whole body is thrown into a motor disturbance. Arms and legs thrash. The whole body is out of control. There is drooling from the mouth. Then the person goes into an unconscious state for 20 minutes or so. When they awake, they have no recollection of what has occurred.

I called for an ambulance and for my sister Jan, then waited close to Nick who was still asleep in our bedroom in the loft which overlooked the living room and family room of our apartment.

When I heard the arrival of the medics, I ran downstairs, frantically flipping on all the lights. "Here we are. Hurry, please!"

The 2 men who had come for him were not very tall. They took one look at my 6 foot, 195-pound husband and hesitated. "How are we going to get him on this cart?" one asked the other. "Maybe he can walk down the steps for us."

I became extremely upset.

Nick was awakened by the discussion. I told him, "You have to go to the hospital, Nick."

Looking dazed, he asked, "What do I have to go to the hospital for?"

"You just had a seizure."

"No, I didn't! I'm not going to any hospital!"

I pointed to an abrasion on his leg. "See that mark on your leg? You got that from kicking the bed during the seizure." Nick was reluctant, but consented to go.

I was confused, in shock and disbelief. The bubbles had been floating everywhere, the happy merry-go-round music was playing, and all of a sudden the bubbles burst and the music stopped. An ugly black monster arrived on the scene, looming up to cast a dark shadow over all our hopes and dreams.

Jan and Jack arrived at the hospital moments after our own arrival. I dreaded the call I had to make to Nick's parents. I was supposed to be phoning them with happy news about a new baby. Instead I was going to have to awake them in the middle of the night to tell them their only son had a seizure! I experienced so much emotional pain just thinking about it that Jan finally offered to make the calls to our families.

I couldn't seem to get situated in the waiting room chair while Nick was taken for a CT scan. The baby was causing a lot of discomfort. To put in the time, I read pamphlets on seizures and epilepsy. "Wow!" I thought. "My husband must be epileptic! I'm going to have to learn to live through seizures."

Finally, between one and two a.m., one of the attendants came out and told me, "Mrs. Shirilla, there is no intracranial bleeding, and nothing serious showed on his CT scan. But he must stay over night. In the morning his doctor will come in and give you a more detailed report."

I decided to stay all night, too. Uncomfortable as I was, I could not leave Nick. After the others left, I prayed most of the night.

At 8:00 in the morning on May 17, our family doctor

came into our room. "How do you feel, Nick?"

"I feel good."

"What happened last night?" Nick told him all about the seizure.

I sensed the doctor was avoiding the CT scan report, but I HAD to know. "Doctor," I asked, "what did the CT show?" He looked at me with concern. "A mass."

My heart sank deep into my chest and plummeted down into my feet. "A mass?" I echoed.

"Yes, Judy, your husband has a mass on the brain."

"You mean a tumor? A brain tumor?"

I had studied neurology during the second year of nursing school. During that course, I'd learned about brain tumors. Everything about them was ugly. In my mind I had concluded, "This is the worst kind of illness anyone could have."

Until the doctor spoke the word "mass" I had blocked from my thoughts the fact that a grand mal seizure is the chief symptom of a brain tumor. Devastation overwhelmed me.

The doctor continued, "Be assured there will be further studies. I believe it is benign, possibly a meningioma. These are usually curative, but Nick will need surgery. I can recommend several surgeons and you can choose one from the list."

It's amazing how quickly one's hopes and dreams and the excitement of expecting a new baby can be dampened. Our minds swirled with confusion and hopelessness.

We chose a surgeon whose name was familiar to me from nursing school. He was an excellent doctor I had observed as a student nurse as he had performed an evacuation of a hematoma. I had heard wonderful reports about his technique and his sterility and remembered being quite impressed with his skills myself. Also, I'd had an opportunity to hear him speak at one of the annual Cancer Symposiums at the hospital where I worked. He'd seemed exceptionally knowledgeable about brain tumors.

When he came to the hospital to see us, he was completely honest. "I want you to go to Cleveland," he said. "I want Nick to have an MRI." (Magnetic Resonance Imaging) Our local hospital did not have the machine or the necessary technology. We agreed and he made the arrangements.

After we returned from Cleveland, the surgeon sat down with us and explained, "Nick has an astrocytoma. At this time, it is low-grade – probably Grade I or II. And it's probably benign, but we won't know that for certain until we receive the biopsy report." He offered us much hope and guidance. "I will do the surgery," he continued. "I will do a craniotomy and try to remove as much of the tumor as possible as aggressively as possible without causing damage."

The tumor was in Nick's right frontal lobe, and from what the doctors told me that is the safest location. It is considered the desert area of the brain. No speech, hearing, memory, or vital organs would be affected even though the tumor was so large that it was starting to press on his motor area in the center of his brain.

As we planned for the operation, the surgeon warned, "Because Nick is so young, I may possibly recommend some radiation post operatively." Who would have ever dreamt that we would await brain surgery at the same time we were waiting for the birth of our first child?

Ten days overdue and no signs of labor! When I went to my gynecologist, I had to inform him of my husband's circumstances. I sobbed. "I don't know what to do, doctor! I'm supposed to have this baby, and it's not even cooperating at this point! But my husband MUST have surgery!"

My mind was crowded with questions, concerned and anxious thoughts. Would Nick be able to be present to assist with the birth of our child? At Lamaze classes we had prepared to work together mentally, physically, emotionally and spiritually. Now everything was up in the air. Our future seemed to be in the hands of the doctors and nurses who surrounded us day after day. We were at their mercy.

That day my gynecologist said something to me I hadn't heard before. "I talked with the brain surgeon, Judy. I understand that your husband has a Glioblastoma."

"A what?" I felt overwhelmed. Ever since this nightmare had begun, I'd pulled out all my books from nursing school, and any other books I could get my hands on that were related to Neurology and the brain. Everything I had read had told me that with treatment a person who suffered from a Glioblastoma had a life expectancy of 18-20 months maximum.

I cried. My doctor tried to comfort me. "I'll talk with the surgeon, Judy. We'll work something out. Do you want to have this baby tomorrow? You are 10 days overdue. I won't let you go longer than 14 days, but I can induce labor tomorrow."

Still in shock, I mumbled, "I'll think about it."

I called him later that day and suggested, "Possibly Wednesday?" He agreed.

The brain surgeon advised us to postpone Nick's surgery until after the baby was born. He would put my husband on anti-convulsive medicine – Dilantin – so he could participate in the birth of the baby.

I would give birth to my first child in the midst of a major life-crisis. It was time to move into our first new home. On top of this, my husband had a brain tumor!

II.
FIRST CRANIOTOMY SURGERY
(June 15, 1987)

A Dark Cloud Despite the Sun

"Don't hire a moving van," my husband's employers told us. "We'll take care of everything." Wonderful people that they are, they showed up on moving day with the company moving van and 18 hardworking young men. In no time at all we were out of the apartment and into our new home.

On June 3, 1987, at 1:30 in the afternoon, with Nick by my side, I gave birth to a beautiful 8 pound 10 ounce baby boy. It was the most exciting time of our life! Little Nicholas Samuel came into the world like a bundle of joy. Since my dad never had a son - only four daughters, Nick said that we should give our baby my dad's middle name, Samuel. Nick's dad's name is also Nick, so our son was given the name of both grandfathers as well as his father's name. With one eye open and the other one closed, he looked around the room, as if to try to understand what was going on.

My dear older sister Debbie, a nurse in a Neonatal Intensive Care Unit, had been with Nick and me during the delivery. After talking with my husband, Debbie had agreed that she would be in the labor room in the event that he could not be there. I was blessed to have both my sister and my husband with me in the delivery room.

The vaginal delivery took place within 2 ½ hours of the induction of Pitocin. But what pain I had suffered prior to that! Posterior back pain, labor pain, abdominal pain! I learned that for 2 ½ hours I could endure anything. It was worth it all. My son was born and our lives were complete. We were now a family!

My husband was so excited to be present at the birth of his baby boy. He even cut the umbilical cord! Then he went to the waiting room where our parents were and gave them a thumbs up sign. Everything was okay. He had his son.

The surgeon who was to operate on Nick came in to visit me. He explained, "I'm here to congratulate you and Nick, not to discuss the surgery." How we appreciated his compassion and his humanness! I began to trust this man completely.

The second day post partum, I became hysterical. I called my family doctor and sobbed, "I'm so scared! My husband has a brain tumor and I have a new baby. What do I do?"

"Judy, you have to look at the positive things in your life right now."

I asked, "What could be positive? My husband has a brain tumor. He has to have surgery. He might die. What's positive about that?"

He said, "You have a new baby now. Enjoy him."

On Sunday, June 14, we had Nicholas baptized. My mom threw a lovely christening at her home, an outdoor picnic on a bright sunny day. There was one dark overshadowing cloud. The following day had been set as the date for Nick's surgery. Nick was to face one of the most difficult challenges of his life which would begin our journey into the unknown, a journey into a new land called the life of a brain tumor patient. We began that journey trusting God with everything we had.

Determination, the Name of the Game

The surgeon came to Nick's hospital room to escort us

down to surgery. As he talked with Nick, he was so reassuring and comforting. I had full confidence that this man would do a good job. He seemed to have everything under control, yet was so concerned and considerate of our situation. You have to trust your surgeon, especially one who will be opening your husband's skull to do a craniotomy.

The successful surgery lasted for about 6 hours. Eighty to ninety per cent of a 3.0-cm brain tumor was removed from Nick's right frontal lobe. It was mostly benign, Grade I-II, just as the surgeon had thought. Even though there were some pre-cancer cells, we were optimistic.

One of the nurses told me that Nick didn't have to be on any intracranial monitoring nor have any screws put in. He did so well that some of our family members and I were even allowed to visit him in the recovery room. Through the preparatory process of putting on the gown and scrubbing up, I felt weaker and weaker. I thought I was going to pass out! I'd lost all my professional strength as a nurse and had to sit down.

When I entered his room and saw his bandaged head, I thought, *He looks like a victim of a bad motor vehicle accident!* Then I really wanted to pass out!

As I sat by Nick's bed, his nurse called out his vital signs. Pressure was good. Pulse was good. Wonderful as the report was, very little of what she said registered in my mind. It's one thing to be the caregiver and nurse and quite another to be on the receiving end of all that information as a family member of the patient.

Being a nurse made my role as wife of the patient more difficult. I could not be naïve. I could not remain optimistic and positive all the time because I had to face the grim reality of all I knew about brain tumors. I knew the possibility of reoccurrence was great.

I admired my husband's outlook. The old saying, "Ignorance is bless" applies. Just before the operation, Nick said, "Judy, this is nothing. It's going to be like taking a bone out of my finger."

An hour or two before surgery Nick had been laughing and making jokes and dreaming about his next trip to Columbus to watch an Ohio State football game. He was a staunch Buckeye fan. I sensed that his deep love for sports and his involvement in sports would play an important part in keeping him motivated. That would give him the fight and perseverance to never give up. He would want to win.

Love for sports can play an important role in how you cope with all of life's challenges. Also, when you are hit with a serious illness, it is important to discuss openly the signs and phases of the grief process, phases like shock and disbelief, anger, denial, depression and finally acceptance. Immediately after you receive the bad news, your body and emotions automatically go into shock. Following the surgery, we were still somewhere between shock, denial and never ever land.

Soon after he was able to go home from the hospital, Nick took the calendar off the inside of the closet door, turned its pages and made a mark. Then he announced, "Judy, I will be back to work by September." I was amazed at his determination.

He loved his job. That, too, gave him something to look forward to, to focus on and keep fighting for. Believe it or not, he WAS back to work by September, in spite of a course of 30 radiation treatments. He teased, "You had a baby. I had major brain surgery and went back to work before you did!"

I agreed, "That's true, you did!" I didn't return to work until Nicholas was five months old.

Our threesome stayed with my parents while my dad painted the inside of our house. New carpeting made the three bedrooms fresh and pretty. Finally, on June 28, we moved into our beautiful home.

Still, much of our life was taken up seeing doctors. One day when we went to visit the radiation doctor, he was so optimistic. "You know, this is really good news, Nick! Did you know that your brain tumor was almost completely removed?"

Yes, I did know that," Nick replied. "The surgeon had mentioned that he had removed at least 80-90%. He said that's a good success rate." We were thrilled.

The doctor said, "Nick, you don't even need the radiation. But because you're only 28, I highly recommend a follow-up of 30 treatments of external radiation. What do you think?"

Nick said, "I think I want to go with it. I want to do anything to insure that I'm going to be okay."

"Nick, you'll be okay for another 58 years!"

You know what? The next time somebody tells you something like that, get a piece of paper and have them put it in writing. There are no guarantees about anything in this life, are there?

We tried to continue as though life was normal, but both Nick and I realized that our lives would never be normal again. Our schedule would include check-ups, frequent MRIs and doctor visits every 6 months to assure that the tumor had not grown back. As hard as we tried to move forward in a positive manner, as if nothing had gone wrong, his brain surgery was always haunting us from the backs of our minds. Once you have experienced the disappointment and the reality of no longer having excellent health, you live in fear of a reoccurrence.

Our challenge as new parents, as patient and caregiver, was to make every day count, to enjoy every day to the fullest, and to count our blessings. And we did. This increased our faith in God and our love for life.

We began to cherish the little things – the changes of the seasons, the new flowers, the birds and bees, the rain and the streams. Everything had a new and different scent and brought with it a new excitement to be alive.

Nick was a comforting, loving, gentile father. He spent hours admiring our new son as he held him on his chest. In his eyes I could see excitement and love for that baby. The impact of Nick's illness definitely increased the bond the two of them shared – a strong, loving bond that even death would never break. Everyone who came around them sensed the beauty of their father-son relationship.

When Nicholas was 5 months old, I went back to work. I remember the many times I sobbed as I drove home, not knowing why. I'd turn the car radio on and the tears would flow. Looking back, I recognize those were times of releasing my pent-up grief. Tears of sadness. The aftermath.

Often when we went to the doctor for another MRI, he would ask, "Judy, what are you worrying about?"

"Oh, I'm just worried that the tumor might come back."

Then the doctor would reassure me, "He's fine. He's fine." I am convinced that our doctor believed in God, in Nick and in the fact that Nick was cured. The longer the time went on – one year, two, three – I began to believe it, too. I became more hopeful, more secure, more comfortable and relaxed, feeling, "It's okay. Life will be okay again."

Often I reminded myself that even though I'd received the most earthshaking, shattering news any happily married wife could receive, it came at the happiest time of my life. God was good. I remembered often what our family doctor had said to me while I was still in the maternity ward with Nicholas. "Judy, you have to look at the positive things in your life right now." He was right. Along with the awful diagnosis of the brain tumor came the awesome beauty of a new baby. And the joy of having that new baby saved us from despair.

Choose Life

Before Nick became ill I had an opportunity to hear Rabbi Kushner, author of When Bad Things Happen To Good People, deliver a dynamic speech. He said, "I was always a man of great faith. I could help so many people until tragedy happened to me." Isn't this true of all of us? I could always cheer up others, encouraging them to remain positive and keep going. But when tragedy hits home, it's so difficult to practice what you've preached.

Rabbi Kushner had a son who suffered from a disease known as Progeria, which causes premature aging. The Rabbi found himself reading the book of Job and questioning God. "God, why are you doing this to me? Why is this happening to me? I've been a good man. I've been helpful to others." His son died at age 13. Although Rabbi Kushner had a difficult time with this, he was able to use his experience to help others deal with terminal illness. "A dying person worries about pain," he said. "They fear pain. If we can alleviate their pain, we can do them a great justice. The second thing they worry about is the fear of being alone."

I joked that my husband and I didn't have that problem. We were never alone. What was "alone" like? His hospital room became a revolving door every time he had surgery. His room was always filled with family and friends. When he came home, we enjoyed a steady stream of friends, neighbors and co-workers. So many people cared about him and our family. This was a blessing to us.

My sister Jan and her husband had experienced hardship early in her marriage. They lost their first son Brian when he was only six days old. Looking back, I realize I didn't understand the extent of her pain and disappointment. I don't know how supportive I was to her at that time, but her compassion and empathy played an important role in our situation. She was always there, as though she had a mission. She often reminded me, "Judy, when hardships come our way, we can do two things. We can get bitter or we can get better. I always chose to get better."

What wisdom! If you get bitter, you don't grow because bitterness stifles growth. A bitter person misses out on so much joy.

Nick was an ordinary guy living an ordinary life. But he dealt with his illness in an extraordinary way and, as a result, touched the hearts and lives of so many people. That was a blessing because becoming an encourager makes sense out of suffering. If you can see your situation touching the lives of others and bringing change in the midst of their hardship, your own difficult situation becomes purposeful and worthwhile.

I've heard it said in church homilies, "Do not despair... Have hope, for God is always with us... Fear not..." Those are profound words. If we despair and lose hope, especially early on in the game of life, we can lose everything. If we become so fixated on the negatives in our life, they will consume us. If we block out all the positive things around us, look at how much joy we could miss!

Every person has two choices. We can choose life or death. I made the choice to choose life. My husband had the same two choices and he also chose life. Make that choice and you can look at everything around you in a positive light.

When you have hope, you gain faith. Then you can endure suffering beyond measure. I received a bookmark as a gift. On it is a picture of a big, bright sun overlooking a pretty meadow and Romans 8:35-37: *Who shall separate us from the love of Christ? Shall tribulation, or distress, or persecution, or famine, or nakedness, or peril, or sword? As it is written: "For Your sake we are killed all day long; We are accounted as sheep for the slaughter." Yet in all these things we are more than conquerors through Him who loved us.*

That is beautiful! It sums it all up. We have a choice. We have control over how we will respond to everything that happens to us.

A lot of people get angry at adversity. The stages of grief I mentioned earlier include anger. Although anger is a normal phase of grief, it can be the most destructive or the most constructive.

If we allow anger to destroy us and say, "I'm angry that I got cancer. Why did this happen to me? Why do I have to suffer? Why did God will this to me? I choose not to go along with this. I'm angry! I'm angry with God! I'm angry at the disease! I'm angry with the whole world!" – Who suffers? We do. We lose hope and faith. We miss out on the joy of the moment.

The Bible says, "Joy cometh in the morning." It always looks darker at night, but we know light/joy can and will return.

When you deal with your anger, be careful not to let it control you and destroy you. Instead, use anger to motivate you. Get angry at your situation – at your cancer, your diagnosis. Say, "I'm going to do something about this! I'm going to take better care of myself and do everything my doctor tells me to do. I'm going to take the treatments and do well with them. I'm going to get better!" If you practice that and believe it with your whole heart, you will do well.

I am thankful that Nick was not an angry person. He lived with a brain tumor for eight years, but never allowed anger to take over. He never permitted himself to become victimized by what was happening to him.

We never have to become victims to our circumstances. We do not have to settle for anything but the best. God wants the best for all of us, no matter what life throws in our pathway. Remember that sacred Scripture: Nothing shall separate us from the love of Christ.

This has been my philosophy. I will not allow my hardships to separate me from the love of my God or my neighbor. I will choose life!

III.
FIVE GOOD YEARS

Life Goes On

Nicholas was always a good and contented baby – as long as his little tummy was full. Every 2 ½ to 3 hours he screamed for his bottle. Otherwise he was a happy camper.

How aware of the circumstances was this little boy? I believe that children have a sense of what is going on around them at an early age. Perhaps even in the womb he knew something was wrong. But because we, his parents, chose to respond to our circumstances by choosing life and happiness, we gave him the opportunity to do the same thing. Our attitudes contributed much to the shaping of his personality. I thank God for the wisdom, insight and courage to endure life's hardships.

On the day Nicholas was born, his father put a basketball in his hand. As he grew up, the games between the two of them graduated from the little kiddie basketball hoops to the larger Franklin hoops. If Nicholas missed a shot, Nick encouraged him. "Oh, come on! You can do it!"

At first, Nicholas was such a little boy the hoop was far away. He worked hard to push the ball up in the air. When he made a basket, he flung his little arms up in the air and cheered. Then we would cheer for him.

I sometimes worked the three to eleven shift at the hospital and got to bed late. Early in the morning while I was still asleep, Nicholas often came into the bedroom and tugged on my sleeve. "Mommy," he'd say, "ball-ball." The only words that little boy knew at that time were mama, dada and ball-ball. As he grew a little older, he called the game "hoops."

Every time we went somewhere in the car, Nicholas carried his basketball under his arm. If we drove past a 10-foot basketball hoop at a church or a school, he called out, "I want to go to that hoop!" Nick and his son frequented one particular court behind our house at a nearby church. They called it their secret hoop. Nick took him there while I was at work. Later he would tell me, "Daddy took me to the secret hoop."

Two and a half years post brain surgery life was wonderful. Much of the shock had left. The sadness and devastation were not as vivid. Although the possibility of the tumor returning was always in the back of my mind, I refused to dwell on it.

On Valentine's Day I came home from work and found a bottle of Asti Spumante champagne on the kitchen counter. An accompanying note read, "Wake me up. Love, Nick" I awakened my thoughtful romantic husband, knowing he'd remembered that we'd become engaged on Valentine's Day. We toasted and celebrated that special memory.

Suddenly Nick became somber. "Judy," he said, "if you want to have another child, we'd better hurry up and have one."

I thought, "My goodness! What is this urgency to have another child?" I had no problem with his suggestion. From the day Nicholas was born I'd often said, "I want another baby. I want another baby." Pregnancy had been a most beautiful time in my life.

In retrospect, I believe in that tender moment God had spoken through my husband with wisdom and foresight.

Soon I was pregnant again. This time, instead of praying only for a healthy baby, I prayed, "Dear God, I want a healthy baby and a healthy family. The nine months that followed were so different. No stress. No impact of an illness or of moving into a new house.

As I was getting ready to go for a check up the day after my due date, Nick advised, "Bring your suitcase."

"I don't need it," I said. "I don't think I'll be going into labor." Although I did feel the baby was moving into position, I didn't expect anything to happen that day.

As Nick and I sat in the gynecologist's waiting room, an unexpected sensation hit me. I bent over and whispered to Nick, but he continued to read his sports magazine.

"Did you hear what I just said?" I asked him. "I think my water broke."

"What do you want me to do about it?" he asked.

"I don't know. Go get a nurse or something." The doctor's wife works there. She is so sweet. She rushed me into the inner office. I was already dilated 2.0 cm. The doctor made arrangements to send me straight to Emergency.

Nick said, "I'll go get the car and pick you up at the door."

"No, don't pick me up at the door," I told him. "I want to walk. I want to get this labor going."

On our way to the hospital I announced, "I'm not going to be a martyr this time." When Nicholas was born, I took no epidural, only Demerol. I was too scared. "This time I'm not going to be stupid. I'm going to take whatever they give me."

We arrived at the Emergency door at 5:30.

On November 16, 1989 at 7:10 p.m. I gave birth to a beautiful eight pound fifteen ounce daughter. I remember the doctor saying, "You're going to have a big baby. Do twins run in your family?" I got all excited, because I would have loved to have twins.

The doctor added, "Look at you! You're ready to have this baby and you have a big smile on your face."

I laughed. "I won't be smiling for long!" But, you know what? I think I smiled the whole time. The delivery was almost pain free. One mild cramp and she was here. A mother's dream. A little girl in her frilly dresses, laces and bows. I was on an emotional high for four weeks. Nobody could bring me down!

Was Nick a proud daddy? The day Lindsey and I came home from the hospital, there was a sign on our front yard fence: "WELCOME HOME, NEW NEIGHBOR LINDSEY NICHOLE!" All the neighbors had signed it.

He had vacuumed and cleaned the house. Little pink diapers were neatly stacked in her dresser drawer.

Our Thanksgiving and Christmas celebrations were exceptional that year. When you learn that life is temporal, every birthday, holiday and special occasion become more significant. Every day was a day to celebrate with a party and noisemakers and balloons because Nick was alive. Nicholas and Lindsey had a dad.

One great fear nagged at me. Nick was such a proud father. The key chain that held his keys to the car said "DAD." But what if he was driving one day with the children in the car and he had a seizure? I knew that once a person has brain surgery, he is at risk for seizures. I had to pray about that and trust God. I learned to trust Him in ways that I had never trusted Him before.

Nick adored his daughter. One day when I came home from work he was walking around with her on his shoulders. Another day she was sitting on his lap. He saw to it that his children could do nearly everything they wanted to do.

We loved to take family trips. One of our favorite vacation spots was Columbus, Ohio. Nick, the Buckeye fan, liked to go in the springtime to watch the Ohio State spring training. He took the children to the stadium with him and introduced them to Brutus, the mascot.

On one particular trip to Columbus when Lindsey was only five months old, Nick and Nicholas went to the stadium and Lindsey and I stayed behind. We planned to take her with us to the French Market and the zoo. Although she slept through the entire walk through the zoo, we joked that her love for animals must have come from that early exposure.

When Lindsey was 18 months old we went to a Deer Park. She fed the deer with a baby bottle, but Nicholas was afraid of them and ran away.

When we bought our house we hadn't noticed that many

people considered our street a "cut-through." I loved to put the children in the stroller and take them for walks. Several times we were nearly hit by a car. "What if the children go into the street and get hit?" I asked Nick. I tried not to focus on that danger or allow it to consume me with fear, but it was a concern. "Maybe we should sell our house and move into a new house on a quiet cul-de-sac," Nick suggested. "The market for homes is really good right now."

We discussed building a new home as a possibility. Nick's CAT scan in December had revealed no evidence of a reoccurrence. Five years and five months had passed since his surgery. We had saved some money and both were working well. We found a beautiful lot on a cul-de-sac not too far from where we were currently living. Nick said, "Let's go talk to the builder," and we did.

In February of 1992 we put our home up for sale. Our new home would be larger to allow sufficient space for two active toddlers and all their toys and belongings.

Jackie, my youngest sister, and her husband had been unsuccessful in their search for a home. "We love your house," she told me one day. "It's in beautiful condition. Maybe we ought to buy it."

Again, God was with us! We had rediscovered our fantasyland with all its bubbles and merry-go-rounds. Two lovely children ages 2 ½ and 5, happy times and the anticipation of another move. The chaos and distress of the past had been replaced by life in order, the way it should be.

One of my favorite photos in my scrapbook is of Nicholas, Lindsey, my husband and myself at the Holodome in nearby Beaver, Pennsylvania. It's a great place with an indoor pool and a beautiful miniature putt-putt golf course. We went there often between surgeries just to get away and treat ourselves when it felt like the world was beating us up.

Every time I look at that picture I'm reminded of the saying, "Those who have fewer regrets are those who take each moment as it comes for all it is worth."

It's important to take time out. For example, I've learned

to make bubble baths an escape. Sometimes a mom has got to get away, shut the bathroom door, light a candle and play her favorite music while submerging in the luxury of a bubble bath.

Maybe you need to take a walk in the park to collect your thoughts, or go for a bike ride or a drive in the car. You need to take care of yourself when you are under a lot of stress.

Get your rest. Eat properly. We made sure we went out to eat often. My sister Debbie would sometimes take off work and drive Nick and me to his checkup. Then we would go some place nice for dinner, a good way to end a difficult day. In spite of tragedy, life must go on. It's important that we make the best of everything.

IV.
RECURRENCE , SECOND CRANIOTOMY
(May, 1992)

Knocked Off the Merry-Go-Round

Only months after our decision to build a new home, Nick developed little signs that trouble might be returning. At first the doctor suspected his problems might be caused by scar tissue that often forms after an operation. But in May 1992, he was rediagnosed with a recurrent brain tumor.

We were faced with a second surgery. I was in shock and disbelief! My initial response was, "This is a nightmare! How could this be happening to me again? Why is life picking on me again? Why not somebody else, God? I've kept my faith. I've kept my love. I've kept my positive attitude! Nick's been faithful, strong and courageous. Why not somebody else? Didn't the doctor do a good job?"

Do you know what? I never did come up with a good answer other than, "Why not us?" We were knocked off our merry-go-round for a second time, but we faced it head on. I urged Nick to go for a second opinion. We made arrangements to see a well-known surgeon in Pittsburgh, Pennsylvania, over Memorial weekend.

After he examined my husband, he told us, "Whoever did your first surgery did an excellent job, but this definitely is a reoccurrence. It's in the same area."

Reality hit. Nick's problems were not caused by scar tissue. This was a reoccurrence. The surgeon's words were exactly what we needed to hear to get us on the right track. God restored my faith and determination. I concluded, "Our surgeon did a good job. Let him do it again."

The first time through I had been numb, in a state of shock. This time I was more in touch with my feelings. I had some serious concerns and real fears. I thought I had lots of faith since I'd attended kindergarten, grade school and high school in a Catholic school. I had trained for my nursing career in a Catholic hospital. And still I found myself questioning God. "God, is he going to be okay this time? Is he going to come through the surgery okay? Will he be able to be the same kind of father he's always been to our children? Will he be able to play ball with them? Drive a car? Go to work? Talk and walk and think and do all the things he can do now?" — Do you hear the "Doubting Thomas" that was in me?

God knew I needed a revelation. As Nick was about to be wheeled down to the surgical room, I heard someone call, "Judy!" My parents and Nick's turned left to go to the waiting room, but I turned right and walked down the hallway toward the surgery room and the sound of the voice. There I saw my husband's surgeon shuffling about, waiting to go in to prepare for the operation. He extended his arm. I looked at him, shook his hand and said, "Doctor, good luck."

The Lord had revealed an inner strength in me – strength enough to assure the doctor. You know, doctors need encouragement, too. Most doctors put their whole heart and soul into their work. He was a dedicated man who gave hours to his profession.

As I shook his hand, I looked up. Above the surgeon's head I saw a beautiful image of Jesus with his arms ex-

tended. He wore a glowing robe. His face was beautiful!
Above Him was a ray of bright, bright sunlight. I sensed it
was the light of His Presence the Scriptures talk about.
God is our light. Jesus is the light of the world, our guiding
light.

At that very moment, Nick's doctor reached out his arms
and gave me an embrace. In that embrace, I felt the love and
strength of the Holy Spirit. I was given strength in my doubting moment.

As I walked away to return to my awaiting family and
throughout the nearly six hours we sat together, I was at
peace. I continued to pray, knowing that Nick would come
through his surgery okay.

While we waited, I shared my experience with my family.
My mother-in-law said, "I thought I heard a voice calling
you down the hallway." That confirmed for me that the voice
of Jesus had called me aside so He could give me peace.

One of my favorite readings played an instrumental part
in my husband's healing. It is called "Footprints."

"One night, a man had a dream. He dreamed he was
walking along the beach with the LORD. Across the sky
flashed scenes from his life. For each scene, he noticed two
sets of footprints in the sand: one belonging to him and the
other to the LORD. When the last scene of his life flashed
before him, he looked back at the footprints in the sand. He
noticed that many times along the path of his life there was
only one set of footprints. He also noticed that it happened
at the lowest and saddest times in his life.

"This really bothered him, and he questioned the LORD
about it. "LORD, you said that once I decided to follow you,
you'd walk with me all the way. But I have noticed that during the most troublesome times in my life there is only one
set of footprints. I don't understand why, when I needed you
most, you would leave me."

"The LORD replied, "My precious, precious child. I love
you, and I would never leave you. During your times of trial
and suffering, when you see only one set of footprints, it
was then that I carried you."

In the very lowest of times, when I didn't even know if I could go on, the Lord had revealed Himself and said, "He's going to be all right. Trust Me."

On every step of that difficult journey I was able to see God, always there working through other people, having them in the right places at just the right time, helping us to make the right decisions.

Don't ever neglect to recognize that God sends us messengers. It's no accident when someone is there for you when you need support the most or when you realize that, somehow, you've been carried through your ordeal. Those are God-given gifts.

After more than five hours, Nick's surgeon appeared at the door of the waiting room, his face beaded with perspiration. He looked like he had just completed the most difficult, most painful job of his career. I wondered, 'Could it have been that difficult for someone who is as trained and brilliant as he? ...Or was it the outcome that's having its effect on him?"

He bent down and gave my mother-in-law a hug, then hugged me. With a somber look on his face, he announced, "I've removed the tumor, but I cannot promise that it will not come back in six months." He shook hands with my father, my father-in-law and my mother. We thanked him and he turned and left.

At the moment he spoke, I knew I had been handed down somewhat of a death sentence for my husband. Although the doctor hadn't used the word "cancer," I was able to interpret that the tumor had been cancerous and deadly.

How we appreciated the doctor's compassion, knowing that he was in the process of moving his practice and his family to a new location. Under such pressure himself, he could have just brushed us off. Here we were, also in the process of making another move. I knew what it involved.

Nick was so excited about our future new home. We'd been out shopping for carpet the day before he got sick. Several times he and Nicholas went to our future neighborhood to walk through the homes that were being built in that area. I knew we had to decide soon whether or not we were to go ahead and build, but didn't want to be the one to burst another bubble for him. So I prayed, asking God to help us make the right decision. Soon Nick's surgeon said to me, "Judy, if you like your home, if you don't have to move, if there's any way you can get out of your plans to build, I'd recommend that you stay where you're at. Moving is so stressful. There's a lot to do in a new house – painting, wallpapering, putting in a lawn – and I don't know if Nick will feel up to it."

More bubbles burst. Our life was out of order once again. I knew I faced the most devastating time of my life. Again I prayed, "Oh, God, I don't want to be the one to have to tell Nick moving to a new home isn't a good idea."

Early one Sunday morning I awoke and prayed about the situation. I continued to pray on my way to the hospital. While Nick and I were visiting, out of the blue he said, "Judy, I've been thinking. If you wouldn't mind, I don't know if it's a good idea that we move right now. If Jackie and Mike don't mind, I think we should back out of our deal with them. We can help them look for another house. I believe we should just stay where we're at."

I was elated! God had answered my prayers! I gave Nick a big hug.

"You don't mind?" he asked.

"Mind? Not at all! I've been thinking the same thing, but didn't want to have to tell you." How good God is! He always comes through.

Then Nick looked at me with the eyes of a little boy. "Do you think I could put a basketball court in the back yard for Nicholas and me?" He'd been asking for this since Nicholas was small. I'd say, "But, Nick, he's only two years old. He doesn't need his own basketball court." Later he'd ask again. I'd say, "Nick, he's only three. Come on, we're going to spoil this kid!"

This time I realized that having a basketball court of

his own really had been Nick's dream since he was a young boy. I hugged him again and said, "Nick, you can do whatever you want. I don't care. Go ahead and put in that basketball court."

The recurrent tumor finalized so many things for me. Our dreams for a new home were crushed. You look around and see other people building and moving, getting the home they'd always wanted. Our lives were stuck. Not that our home is a bad place to live, but another dream had just been knocked off our happy merry-go-round.

I called the builder and explained our situation to him. He was wonderful about seeing to it that our down payment on the lot was refunded.

I love babies. Although I already had two beautiful children, I'd hoped to have another one. The rude awakening came. We wouldn't have any more children because of the added stress that would bring, now that Nick's health was failing. I guess we're never content with what we have at the moment.

St. Paul said, "Whatever state I am in, therewith I shall be content." I have learned over the years to be content with what I have and where I am. It was a hard lesson to learn, through many trials and tribulations.

V.
FIRST RADIATION IMPLANT
(July 9, 1992)

THIRD CRANIOTOMY, to remove scar tissue

(January, 1993)

Journey in a Strange Land

1992. I was 32 years old. My husband was 33. We were at the prime of life, but realizing that we were faced with a terminal diagnosis. I wondered how well we would do.

During the days following Nick's surgery I wandered throughout the hospital, talking to anyone who would listen and listening to anyone who would offer hope. Many days I found myself in the chapel, praying and praying and praying. "God, what do I do? How do I get through this?" Instead of looking forward to the building of a new home, we faced cancer. A strange new journey had begun.

One day I went to the chaplain's office and asked him, "Father, why is this happening to us? I know that God wills us suffering to strengthen us and draw us closer to Him. I know it must be His will for my husband to have cancer. But what do I do now?"

Father held up his hand and stopped my searching for answers. "Judy, God's will is not so much that He wills us suffering and that Nick is being punished. Evil exists in this world and takes its toll. But God promises He will be there for us in our times of great despair."

I continued like I never had before to ask the Lord for courage, strength and hope.

Our doctor was so supportive, despite the weight of his own life situation. He cried with us. He told me, "Judy, I thought I'd cured Nick."

I responded, "You did heal him to be able to live for five years, Doctor. Nick's had a wonderful, normal life. He's been able to continue in his job. He's done all the things he loved to do. He played basketball with his son, and played with his daughter. He drove a car. He functioned in a normal capacity without any deficit. That was a blessing. That was a healing. But only God has the capacity to heal someone forever."

"But, Judy, what is five years?"

"Five years means a lot. Nicholas will always remember the daddy, the special friend, the BEST friend who shared the first seven years of his life. Lindsey always will have an image of being daddy's little girl and a memory of who her daddy was."

We were faced with some difficult decisions to make concerning Nick's follow-up treatment. I had read that chemotherapy is not effective for brain tumors because it does not cross the blood brain barrier. Yet the oncologist planned one year of chemotherapy.

Would this be the most effective and the best treatment? This was another factor to take before the Lord in prayer.

On the day of my husband's discharge from the hospital, I pleaded with the surgeon, "Please, I want the best follow-up possible for Nick. I'll take him anywhere in the state, anywhere in the country - anywhere I have to to get him better. Please, do you know of ANYBODY? Are there any treatments in the field that offer hope at this time?"

I detected the sadness in his eyes. In a low-pitched tone of concern, he said, "I can give you the name of a neurosurgeon who is doing a very new and innovative procedure called radium implant. I can call him and recommend Nick as a referral."

I felt hopeful again. My husband would have a second chance. "God, you've given us a second chance!"

Soon after that, I saw a cartoon in our local newspaper. It was created by Bill Cane, author of Family Circus. He wrote, "Yesterday is the past, tomorrow is the future, but today is a gift. That is why it is called 'the present.'"

The day I learned about radium implants was certainly a gift. I thought, "Nick's been given a second chance and every day that he lives beyond "today" is a gift from God. It's special!" A new and positive hope welled up in me. When I shared this insight with Nick, he became more hopeful, too.

The morning after he was discharged from the hospital, only a few days shy of Nicholas' fifth birthday, Nick had his friends plow up our yard. The completed basketball court is huge. Nick engraved in the concrete, "To Nicholas. Love Mom and Dad." He said, "I want my son to practice hard. Some day I want to see him play in the N.B.A."

Lindsey loves to ride her bike and twirl her baton on the concrete.

We met with the doctor recommended by Nick's surgeon. He put it on the line. He said, "The tumor is Grade III or IV. These can be deadly. You need immediate treatment."

"But, Doctor," I asked, "other doctors have told us that if a person has to have a tumor, Nick's is in the best location and the safest area. Okay, it's still bad. So what can you do?"

"Well, if he's willing, Nick is a candidate for a radiation implant. We would place radiation right at the site of the tumor with tiny little catheters. This would kill any of the remaining cells. It's his best hope for a cure."

Nick and I were excited! There was hope for a cure! The doctor reminded us, "Don't push aside the severity and seriousness of his condition."

We cried the whole trip home. We were devastated. ...And we weren't even sure that we liked that bearer of grave news. He was so cold and impersonal – and honest.

But, do you know what? What other way is there but to tell someone the truth. "You have cancer and it's bad. It's in your brain and we have to kill it. We have to get it out of there. We have to destroy it quickly." Forthrightness causes the hearer to snap into action.

For our anniversary in June Nick took me to a place called "Tara, The Country Inn" for a couple of days. We kind of "escaped," got away from it all. There we regrouped and decided we would ask for the radium implant to be done. Journeys into new lands are not always comfortable and fun.

A Halloween Monster

On July 9, 1992, Nick was implanted with six catheters. For five days he was in isolation. We had to stay at least ten feet behind a big lead radiation shield and could only remain in his room for ten-minute intervals. Can you imagine the feelings of isolation my husband experienced? The dark cloud of cancer hovering over him, the loneliness – he had to have felt like he had the plague! Somehow he determined that all this would not get him down.

Thank God for sisters! Jan, Debbie and Jackie faithfully stayed with me during all the surgeries. They packed a cooler with all kinds of food. They constantly encouraged Nick's family and our children. We cried together and laughed together. We took treats to Nick since he wasn't fond of the hospital food. As a matter of fact, he hated it.

"Bring me a cheeseburger from McDonald's," he often teased. "How about a Big Mac?"

Nick's implant surgery went well. He recovered and returned to his job in September. I must admit that I did have a little fear. He worked on a big machine. That could have been dangerous. I voiced my concern to one of his bosses.

His employers got together and discussed his situation and promptly transferred him to assist as an inspector. Nick's employers were instrumental in providing for Nick's needs, helping him continue to feel needed. Their kindness and generosity meant a lot to us.

We had been warned that complications might accompany the radium implant. One was scar tissue. "Scar tissue?" I'd said to myself, then asked, "Doctor, what are you going to do if he gets it?"

"We can ride it out with medication," he explained. "Sometimes, if it's bad enough, it requires surgery, but we won't go that route unless we have to."

August went well. September went well. October went well ... until Halloween night when a scary monster attacked us. Nick had a seizure while standing at the kitchen sink. Small focal seizures involving his facial muscles occurred again and again.

The next morning, I reported off work and called the surgeon.

"Okay, I need to see him," he said. I took him in and they ran tests. Something showed up on his MRI. A 4.0-cm mass!

"We're not sure what the mass is," I was told. "It may be a tumor or it may be scar tissue." They opted to treat him with steroids, the treatment of choice for scar tissue.

Steroids shrink the swelling in the brain which is like a small compartment. If it gets too many things in it, like a sandwich bag that's been stuffed too full, it could pop. They had to shrink the swelling to allow room for the brain to function normally.

"Nick will probably need another operation," the doctor reminded me during one of our visits. "Only a miracle could prevent that."

I insisted, "But I believe in miracles. They happen every day. Why couldn't Nick be a miracle?"

"Well, he could, but come the first of the year, he is probably going to need surgery to remove whatever is in there." I continued to be hopeful, but realistic.

By December, the mass had grown larger and pressed on his motor area. He WOULD have to go through a fourth surgery, his third within a five-month period – the craniotomy in May to remove the second tumor, the implants in July, and now a second craniotomy to remove whatever was there. As we faced the first surgery I had been hopeful but in shock. The second time I was still hopeful, but scared – and scared again for the implants. Facing his fourth, I was SCARED TO DEATH!

Some Day...

I tried to stir up hope, remembering God's promise found so many times in the Scriptures, "Do not despair. Have hope, for I am with you." Somehow He continued to carry my family and me through the ordeal, always sending the best doctors and surgeons, the best nurses and, of course the best family, co-workers, friends and neighbors that anyone could ask for.

The time spent in the waiting room felt uncomfortably familiar. Finally the phone rang. I answered and immediately recognized the voice of the surgeon. As he reported the results of Nick's surgery, I sobbed vigorously.

"Judy, what is the matter?" he asked. "This is good. Nick doesn't have a recurrent brain tumor. The mass was all scar tissue. He'll do much better now."

"These are tears of joy and relief, Doctor," I sobbed.

Our neighbor, who had been waiting with us, came to my side with an expression of intense fear on his face. "Judy, what's the matter?" I explained what the doctor had reported and the reason for my tears. He said, "Seeing you cry so hard shook all of us!"

Now, once again, we could get on with our lives.

One of my goals was to connect with people in situations similar to my own. Whatever your hardship, whatever your struggles, find someone else you can bond with.

Throughout all of Nick's illnesses we sought others who had brain tumors. We had an inner yearning to find out how they were coping, what surgery did they have, what helped them? Just to be able to interact with them gave us hope and strength. They helped us realize we were not alone in our struggles.

Nick recovered so well. Janice suggested that we get involved in a support group and did some research for us. She found a support group in our local area called HOPE – Helping Ourselves Physically and Emotionally. We needed that kind of support!

Nick had asserted, "I don't really need a support group.

They removed the tumor and now I'm doing fine. I don't have cancer any more." But the reality was that, once you've had cancer, it could always come back.

Joining that group was a great asset to our lives. We met a lot of other patients who were undergoing various treatments and surgeries for all kinds of cancers. At the close of each meeting, the coordinator gave us little "angel cards" printed with inspiring messages of hope. We would hold hands and say together, "We are not alone, and we're all going to make it." And we did. We made it! We walked the road together and we made it, and experienced a lot of joy and fun in the process. We proceeded with life. –What else could we do?

I urge everyone who is going through a difficulty, be it divorce, illness or loss of a job, to seek out people who are in your shoes and walk with them. We met a lot of wonderful people, like John who had the same doctor Nick had.

John, from St. Louis, was 33 years old. He was one of the first patients to receive a radiation implant. John was helpful to Nick because he had already gone through what Nick was going to face. Instantly the two men developed a strong friendship.

In September, Nick was doing well, but John had to be hospitalized. When we learned his dad would be flying him to the hospital, we decided we would drive there to meet him. I teased Nick. "I have to meet this guy in person. The first thing I'm going to ask him is, 'Are you a good eater?'"

Nick was a picky eater. He would be happy with a hamburger every night. But I love to cook big meals with lots of vegetables. I wanted to ask John his views about what causes cancer. I often wondered if the cause could be the water we drink, the food we eat or the air we breathe. I was certain that omitting lots of vegetables from the diet must be a cause.

John was a tall, handsome young man with dark hair. Soon after we'd entered his hospital room, I asked him, "John, are you a picky eater? What types of foods do you eat."

"Oh, I eat everything. I eat fish and shrimp, meat and

potatoes. I eat vegetables. You name it." There went my theory!

I reconciled to the fact that cancer is something that exists and we were unfortunate enough to be affected. Nick read somewhere that the chances of getting a brain tumor are one in 180,000. He quipped, "My chances of hitting the lottery are greater than that!"

We don't have a choice. We have to take whatever comes our way.

I had talked with a minister at our hospital who had just lost his wife. I extended my sympathy to him, told him about our situation and asked if he would mind praying for Nick. He said, "Judy, I am going to tell you something. We are all dealt a hand of cards and we have to play it. Whatever hand we get, no matter how lousy it is, we must play it to the best of our ability."

Many times people we knew said to me, "Judy, you're so strong. How do you do it?"

I always answered, "What choices do I have? You are dealt this hand and you must play with whatever you are dealt.

I believe Nick always had an inner sense of an early death, because at one point early in our marriage he'd said to me, "I don't see myself growing old."

I became angry. "Why do you say that? There's a lot of beauty in growing old with someone you love."

"I know that, but I just don't see myself growing old."

As we continued family activities after the surgery, Nick was the best father any two children could have. He savored every moment he spent with his children. "Look, Judy," he said as he watched Lindsey interact with her younger cousins one day. "Isn't she beautiful? Look how she loves babies!" Then he became somber. "Some day, I'm not going to be here. Lindsey is going to grow up and get married and have babies of her own, and I'm not going to be here to see it happen." He paused again. "And Nicholas is going to be such a good athlete, but I'm not going to be around to see it." My heart ached.

I hugged him and replied, "Yes, you ARE going to be here. And just in case you're not, realize that you've already seen Lindsey's love for children and for animals. You've seen Nicholas' love for children and sports. God allowed us to see this at an early age."

We continued to live our lives one day at a time. As I bathed the children or unwound from a busy day, in quiet moments, uncontrollable tears flooded down my face.

"Daddy, Mommy is crying again," Lindsey would tell her father. Nick would come and hold me tight. "Judy, you have to find some humor in life. You can't cry all the time."

I wondered, "What is so funny?" Then Nick would say something silly and we'd all laugh.

Close to Christmas, just as Nick and I were leaving for his check up, Nicholas wrapped up his favorite coloring book and crayons. He said to Nick, "Daddy, these are for you."

I was so touched that tears rolled down my cheeks. I teased, "Where is my gift?"

Our son explained, "You'll get yours next year, Mommy. You're not the one who is sick now." He knew his father needed special attention and little Lindsey did, too. She fussed over her daddy all the time. They kept him going, I'm sure. He had a lot to live for.

A parent's normal coping mechanism includes protecting your children from harm by hiding the painful aspects of life from them. Nick and I chose to always be honest with our children. We allowed them to be informed and involved as much as possible by sharing in making our decisions. We all wanted to believe that Nick would beat the problem, but at the same time ...what if he didn't?

Just by living in the same household, children sense what is going on. To block them out, to ignore them, to pretend that nothing is wrong intensifies their fears. What they imagine can be far worse that what is actually happening.

I explained to Nicholas and Lindsey, "Daddy has a boo-boo and the doctors have to insert special medication to get rid of his infection." They accepted that. I told them, "Daddy has an awful disease called cancer and needs treatment to help get rid of it.

One day when I came home from work I noticed pictures of Nick after his first brain surgery lying on our dresser. "Why are these out?" I asked Nick.

"Oh, I was showing Nicholas and Lindsey the pictures my dad took when my head was all bandaged."

"Why would you be showing them those? It's been five years." Then I thought, "Maybe he doesn't feel good today and he felt a need to share with them and prepare them for what might happen.

Nick loved to wear a T-shirt with the athletic logo "CONVERSE" written across the front. Underneath that word it said, "It's what's inside that counts." We often used that slogan in our conversations.

One day when Lindsey was not quite three and Nicholas was five, the two were engaged in a heavy debate. I heard Nicholas say, "Daddy's boo-boo is gone."

Lindsey retorted, "No it isn't. I still can see it."

Her older brother responded, "But it's not what is on the outside that counts. It's what is on the inside."

After his radiation treatments, when he started to lose his beautiful, thick wavy hair, he would quip, "You know, there's a lot of advantages to having no hair. It doesn't take me as long in the shower. I just stroke the wash cloth across my head one time and my hair is clean. I don't even have to use a comb!" We bought him one of those huge plastic Bozo combs. He loved it!

A beautician friend once told him, "Don't ever feel bad that you're bald. Baldness is beautiful. God only created some men with perfect heads. The rest He covered with hair."

He'd always worn a baseball cap, but after he lost his hair, he quit wearing one. "Aren't you going to wear your cap today?" I'd ask him.

"Nah. I want people to see my incision." The incision started by his eyebrow and ran all the way to the back of his head like a question mark. I think going without a cap was his way of accepting his own illness. Seeing is believing.

I imagine he thought, "With a hat covering the scar, I don't look sick, I don't act sick. I have no deficit and I'm not wobbly. I'm not talking weird and I'm not forgetful, but I DID have surgery. I had brain surgery, do you see the evidence?"

At the time of his re-diagnosis, he'd wept – the first time I'd ever seen him cry. He told my sister Jan, "I just can't believe I got this back! I don't want anybody else raising my children. I don't want Judy to ever get remarried if something happens to me."

Jan replied, "Well, Nick, I can understand why you feel the way you do. But think of all the quality time that you've spent with Nicholas and Lindsey. How many fathers live to be 50, 60, 70 and never show the love, joy, concern and compassion that you have shown for your children? The quality of life that you give them is so rich that they'll never forget you. Even if Judy does go on with her life, and your children go on with theirs, you are her husband and their father and always will be." Nick smiled.

One day, as the children were getting into our van, they were fighting like two little monsters. "I want to sit there!" "No! I was here first!" Nick and I looked at each other and I started to laugh.

"Now, really, Nick, do you think anybody is going to want me with two children who act like this?"

He laughed too. "I guess I don't have a thing to worry about, do I?"

That incident was the beginning of an ongoing joke. Not long after that, he saw a guy the world would consider "dorky" and he said to my sister Jackie, "If something happens to me, you fix Judy up with somebody like that." His pain and his love for me were evident, but I knew that he would want his family to have someone dear some day. I knew that he believed that was God's will, but it was not an easy thing for him to voice.

He used to say things like, "If something happens to me, will you stay in this house?"

I'd respond, "Probably. I don't know. But, Nick, nothing is going to happen to you."

'I thought, "What a unique way my husband has of dealing with his situation and his love for his family." He never complained, "Why did this happen to me? Am I a bad person?" He never voiced his anger and frustration to any greater degree than to say with gentleness, "You know, some day I may not be here." I admired him for that.

He was such a good husband. He cut the grass, took care of the cars, paid the bills and helped with the kids. He allowed me to do whatever I wanted. Sometimes he'd tease, "You know, you're not going to survive without me."

I told him, "You know what? You're right, so you can't die!"

He picked up his burden and he carried it, smiling even through the difficult painful times. He always thought of the positive aspect of his situation. Many times I heard him say, "I might be one of those people who will beat this." We all shared that hope.

Creating Memories

Someone once gave me a little card that said, "Relax. God is in charge." It feels so nice when we're able to lay back without worrying about a thing. But sometimes, we don't want to give up all the control to Him and so we worry and fuss. I tried not to do that. I tried to keep our lives as normal as I could.

"How do you do it, Judy?" people asked. "You never lead a normal life."

Many times I explained, "If I had married a famous baseball player, my life would be one of living in hotel rooms and traveling to and from baseball games in various cities. That's not a 'normal' life either." I was the wife of a brain tumor patient. I did it. I was there for him and never thought of doing otherwise.

To us, normal was going to the hospital for MRIs on an average of every 2 ½ to 3 months, never more than six months between appointments. The doctor wanted to keep a close watch on Nick because the tumor could start growing at any time. Normal included weeklong stays in the hospital. We learned to live "between check-ups," seeing to it that every day counted.

Humor played an important part in helping us "lighten up" to get through the tough times. Nick and our six foot eight inch tall neighbor played a lot of personal jokes on one another. One time while we were away, he came over and took a bolder out of the island in front of our house and carried it over to his property. We noticed it was missing as soon as we drove into the driveway. "What happened to that rock?" I asked Nick.

He laughed. "Oh, it's probably next door. He's going to get a hernia playing pranks like that!" The next day Nick would hide something of his.

That same neighbor and I both enjoyed gardening. Often when we got together he and I compared notes. Every day, as soon as he got home from work, he'd entered his front door, exit through the back door and go out to inspect his garden.

One day, Nick came home carrying little patio tomatoes in a basket.

"What are those for?" I asked him. "I have tomatoes in our garden that will be ripe soon. Besides, you don't even like tomatoes!"

"I'm going to play a joke on our neighbor." Nick tied those little tomatoes on all the tomato plants in the garden next door.

When he came home from work, we were sitting on our patio, watching to see what would happen. As usual, he paused outside his back door to inspect his prized garden from a distance. We heard him say to his sons, who were playing in the yard, "Look, boys! Look, I've got red tomatoes!" He ran to the edge of his garden.

Seeing the strings that attached the tomatoes to the plants, he looked in our direction and asked, "Nick, did you do that?" We shared a lot of good times, a lot of humor, a lot of friendship. That, too, helped us keep going and made life exciting.

In June 1993, we were blessed beyond our dreams. My brother-in-law said to us, "Why don't you use my frequent flyer tickets to take the kids to Florida to visit Disney World?" We'd never thought about such a trip because our children were so young.

My husband's cousin heard about the offer and told us, "We have a condominium in Haines City near Orlando. You could use that for a week. It's right on a golf course." Another brother-in-law gave us money to pay for the kids' airline tickets. How could we say no?

Although Nick was weak, he was still able to enjoy our vacation. We saw Beauty and the Beast, one of Lindsey's favorite stories. We saw the Ninja Turtles, the Caravan and the Little Mermaid. The kids rode the teapot with their dad. Our week at Disney World created some lasting memories.

But you don't have to go somewhere far away to create memories. You can do it right at home. That's important because no one can take memories away from you. What you cherish in your heart is there forever.

I think of Nicholas' fifth birthday, a difficult birthday because Nick just had another reoccurrence. But we had a party anyway. Nick bought him a beautiful blue bicycle with training wheels. Nick's boss's wife Illene wanted to do something special to cheer us up. She hired a clown to visit the party. The kids loved him and so did the adults. Laughter is great therapy. We'll never forget that day!

VI.
THIRD RECURRENCE
(August 17, 1994)

SECOND RADIATION IMPLANT
(September 15, 1994)

A Brush with Death

One day in August of '94 Nick and Nicholas came home from riding bikes in time for Nick to cut the grass. I was in the back yard pushing Lindsey on the swing. Nick had no more than started to mow than he shut the mower off and came to the swing. "My mind is swirling," he told me. "I want to cut the grass, wash the car and..."

"Honey, slow down!" I said. "Do one thing at a time. What you don't get done, you can finish later."

He smiled, finished cutting the grass, then went into the house and took a shower. When I went in, I found him sitting in his favorite chair, staring into space as if he'd forgotten what he was doing. I realized something wasn't right and promptly called his surgeon.

He said, "He's due for another MRI anyway, so bring him in." The MRI showed a third recurrence.

I asked him, "Can I take him for a second opinion? Maybe there's something new they're doing by now."

He said, "There are so many ways to go about this, Judy. I highly recommend a second implant. That's the best way to treat these tumors. He did well with the first one, but we'll be really aggressive this time, so he'll have more trouble healing."

We did go to Pittsburgh, Pennsylvania for a second opinion. I asked the doctor, "What would you do if it was your brain?"

He laughed. "I'd get a bottle of Jack Daniels and head for the beach.

Oh, how I wanted to head for the beach! But I couldn't run. I couldn't leave Nick. We had to face this head-on. Together. We opted to have the second radium implant.

When we returned home, I explained to our son, "Nicholas, Daddy got his tumor back. They call it 'cancer.' I don't know if you've ever heard the word, but it's a bad illness. It's something that sometimes goes away but then comes back. Often it takes people's lives."

Nicholas interrupted me. "No, Mommy. This one won't take Daddy's life. At least he doesn't have AIDS like Magic Johnson!" To him AIDS was a much worse disease, so he kept his hope high.

Lindsey was only four and a half. It was difficult for her to understand the seriousness of her daddy's illness and the impending consequences.

In September, Nicholas started first grade and Lindsey entered preschool. I was heartbroken that I couldn't share that momentous experience with them. Thank God for my mom! She took over for me in this instance, just as she had taken care of the children so many times before.

I often felt as though my life was out of control and the children were being shuffled around from one set of caring hands to another. But the important thing was that they knew they were loved. No matter who they were with – Grandma Tony or Pa, Nana or Papa, Aunt Debbie or whoever – they always felt safe and loved. We always have to look at the positive aspects of a difficult situation. Nick, our children and I were blessed with the continuous support of our family.

Nick had his fifth brain surgery on September 15, 1994, one of the largest radium implants his surgeon had ever done. Thirteen catheters were implanted at the site of his tumor.

For five days we were separated again, but this time the isolation was not quite as devastating. The hospital had installed a vision screen inside a structure that looked like a phone booth. We could go in the booth and pick up the phone. Nick could turn his television to channel 4 and actually see and talk to the children and me.

I asked the hospital staff if there was any help available for our children to assist them in facing the future. A child-life specialist worked in a playroom where the children could go and color and play while they talked with her. She told them, "It's sad that your daddy is sick. You need to say to yourselves, 'Yes, Daddy is sick and we all feel sad, but what can we do to feel better?'"

She told me, "Your children are adjusting well. Do whatever you can to let them have fun. Maybe you can go to McDonald's or to Chuck E. Cheese and play some games" That is how we dealt with life.

Often God prepares us for tough times by sending special people into our lives. Back in April 1994, I was caring for a young man named Joe at the hospital where I worked. Joe'd had a lung tumor removed. I observed the stressful expression on his wife's face and felt I needed to talk with him. The first spare moment I had, I went into his room and said, "Joe, my husband had a brain tumor and he's done well. Now he's back to work."

He brightened. "Wow! A brain tumor! And he was able to return to his job?" Hearing other people's stories can strengthen and encourage a person.

A bond of friendship was formed between Joe, his wife and myself. I told her that if she ever needed to talk to call me. They had a little boy who was five years old.

Several months later I heard that Joe was in the hospital and not doing well. On August 18, 1994, I called her to find out how Joe was doing. She was crying. "Judy, Joe died this morning."

"I'm so sorry. Yesterday Nick had a reoccurrence."

She said, "Judy, I'll be there for you." We wept together.

From that time on, she was always there when I needed her. She had already been through what I was about to live through.

Soon after Nick came home from the hospital he began to talk about going back to work. Work had become therapy for him. He'd worked for the same company for 15 years. They had developed into a close-knit group. I replied as gently as I could. "You know, Nick, I don't know if you're going to be able to return to work this time. God may be calling you to do a different kind of work now." I knew he was hurt by my words.

September went well. By October his wound still hadn't healed. We'd been warned that there would be side effects and slow healing from receiving such a large amount of radiation, but hearing it and experiencing it are two different things.

My poor husband! The tissue on his head was so thin that stitches kept bursting open. Then fluid leaked out. Each time I'd have to rush him to emergency to have the wound re-stitched.

The fourth time occurred on a Saturday morning in the middle of October. I had been up all night putting dressing after dressing on his wound – even re-enforcing the dressings. Each dressing would quickly be saturated with cerebral spinal fluid.

"He's running a high risk of infection," I thought to myself and phoned the hospital. Similar calls were necessary so frequently that the moment they heard my voice they recognized who was calling. I explained, "My husband's wound is draining. I've been changing the dressing every hour."

The welcome voice on the phone said, "I think you're going to have to bring him here to the clinic in the morning. We'll have to put in a temporary drain to allow his wound to dry out and heal."

That's not what Nick wanted to hear. He didn't want to think about going back to the hospital for any reason, especially while he was still suffering from the side effects of the radiation. He was still on Decadron to keep the swelling down and prevent the scar tissue from causing problems. But the dosage was so high his eyes dried out and, for the first time, he was in pain. A severe headache interfered with his sleep. He spent hours of torment sitting in his chair.

Early that Saturday morning, Nicholas had awakened and overheard the discussion as Nick and I made plans. "Nick, you're going to have to go back to the hospital," he heard me tell his dad. "Nicholas has his first flag football game for his school today. I can ask my father to take you or I can see if my sister will take you. Or I could take you and they could go to the game with Nicholas."

"Mom," Nicholas interrupted, "I want you to go to the game with me. I don't want anybody else taking me." He spoke in such an emphatic tone of voice; I could read between the lines. He was really saying, "If Daddy can't come to my first football game, then I want you there."

I knew I HAD to be there. I called Nick's parents, feeling so guilty. They had planned to go to Columbus for the Ohio State game that day, but willingly altered their plans to take their son to the hospital.

I promised them the moment Nicholas' game was over I would jump in the car and meet them at the hospital. My sister Debbie went with me to the game.

Nicholas did well. In fact, one of his coaches patted him on the back and said, "Good game, Nick." I was so happy to hear him say that! God was good. He allowed Nicholas to play well so he could give his Dad a good report.

My brother-in-law came to the game to report that things weren't going so well for Nick, so I spent most of the time on the phone and missed some of the game. Even though my dad and my sister and brother-in-law were there, Nicholas kept looking for me. Sometimes even our best effort doesn't seem good enough.

I told Nick on the phone, "Honey, if you don't want to wait for me to get there, go ahead and have the drain put in. I'll get there as soon as I can."

The doctor had warned, "Nick, there is a serious risk of meningitis, since this is an open wound." My husband opted for the doctors to proceed with the insertion.

When Debbie and I arrived at the hospital, what we found was not a pretty sight. My husband was curled up in a fetal position, looking very sick and dejected.

I wanted to spend the night with him, but he said, "You go on home and get some rest. Mom and Dad are going to be here with me."

By Sunday morning, I was excited. The children were going with me to see their dad and help me decorate his room. My mom was making cavatelli and meatballs and we were going to take some with us. Nick loved cavatelli.

There is a movie called Hope Floats. Our hopes were floating – up, down, up, down. A hint of our merry-go-round happiness had returned.

Debbie, the children and I arrived at the hospital and rushed to Nick's room. There was a big red crash cart outside the door. "What's happened?" I cried out. "Of course, this isn't here for my husband, is it?" I turned to my sister. "Would you go in there for me and see what happened?"

She entered Nick's room while the children and I waited in the hallway. When she returned, she was white as a ghost. "Judy, you'd better go get the nurse. You'd better find out what happened. He's sleeping, but he looks awful. He's on oxygen."

I searched for his nurse and she explained that while they were draining off some of the fluid, they neglected to put on an occlusive dressing and air was sucked in. He suffered a grand mal seizure which resulted in temporary paralysis. They were preparing to transfer him to the Intensive Care Unit. Our hope sunk!

I was devastated! Just devastated! How could this have happened? We came to decorate his room and enjoy watching him eat cavatelli. All our plans were ruined.

I began making phone calls to our family, telling everybody the situation and suggesting that they come because, once again, his condition was touch and go.

He did perk up that night. The medication pulled him through. But still he faced an uphill climb in the days ahead. The doctor explained that there was so much "stuff" in his head – scar tissue, a tumor, swelling, and now air. Again, I pictured a plastic sandwich bag packed so full it was ready to pop. There was danger of herniation of the brain that could have resulted in a stroke. He was fortunate that didn't occur.

The days that followed were grim. He became lethargic, his blood pressure was low and he quit eating so I spoon-fed him Jello and forced him to take sips of anything. His headaches were so severe they caused vomiting and profuse perspiring. My nurses training told me he was the clinical picture of meningitis.

The Battle Rages

I actually stood guard at the door of his room since the residents were more than ready to do some kind of surgery. More than once I asked a resident who entered, "What are you doing here?"

One replied, "We're going to do plastic surgery. His wound isn't healed."

"I don't think that is an issue right now," I retorted. "I think the issue is a little more serious. We need to worry about this drain first and what we're going to do about that."

One day, twelve hours dragged by without anyone bothering to check on him. Several times I walked to the nurses' station and begged, "Please, can one of the residents check on my husband? I don't think that drain is working properly. He's showing too many symptoms that it isn't doing what it's supposed to do."

No one came. No one called. Finally I went to the pay phone. Acting as though I was calling from home, I paged a neurosurgical resident.

"Who are you?" he asked.

"I'm actually at the hospital. My husband is lying here, going down the tubes with all kinds of symptoms, and nobody has bothered to check on him for twelve hours!"

"I'm sorry," he said. "I'm very busy here in Emergency."

I had never been so angry and upset. I said, "Listen, if you don't come to see my husband now...! This is a life-threatening emergency, too! I understand that you're busy, but this is SERIOUS! Nobody has seen him all day. If something happens to him tonight, and he dies as a result of negligence, I will hold you responsible."

"I will be there as soon as I can."

In the meantime, one of Nick's friends from work came to visit. He couldn't believe how lethargic and unresponsive Nick was.

Finally, the resident arrived and ordered an x-ray of Nick's head.

The next day I phoned the surgeon, but he never returned my call. Every time I called, I was told I couldn't talk to him. *This is absurd!* I commented to myself and said to his secretary, "Then could I please come see him?"

"He's going to be busy seeing patients today. This is his clinic day."

"You don't understand!" I told her. "My husband has been his patient for almost three years. He is very serious and critical. I think he should talk to me!" When I arrived, I was told to sit in his office and wait my turn!

He called me in first and explained, "Your husband needs surgery. I'm putting him on the schedule for tomorrow."

"But, Doctor, you don't understand! My husband's had five surgeries already. He was strong enough to withstand those, but he's so weak this time." I had a gut feeling. Remembering the saying, "Follow your heart," I continued, "I just don't think he can go through an operation and make it. He hasn't eaten. He's been so sick. He hasn't slept properly. I'm worried about pneumonia or blood clots."

"It will take a miracle for him not to have surgery before he leaves the hospital."

"You know what, Doctor? I believe in miracles!"

"It's not what you want, Judy. It's what he wants." I

thought, "Oh, my gosh! He IS taking Nick to surgery!" I prodded the surgeon for Nick's prognosis.

Finally he said, "The brutal reality is that Nick will not be here next Christmas."

I was so angry I wanted to scream! *Who the heck was he telling me my husband wouldn't be here next Christmas? He's not God! He doesn't know that! He can't possibly know that!*

I was scared to death! And confused. When I returned to Nick's room, I looked at the man in the bed next to him who'd also had brain surgery and said, "what should I do?"

He said, "I reckon you'd better call on the Lord."

"That's exactly what I'm going to do. Thank you. Thank you."

There is a beautiful verse at the end of Isaiah 40 that says, *"They that wait upon the Lord shall renew their strength. They shall mount up with wings like eagles. They shall run and not be weary, they shall walk and not faint."* Whenever a new crisis hit, my prayers usually accelerated.

My time "waiting upon the Lord," increased immensely in the coming days. This was the closest my husband had come to dying and the confusion of the experience nearly pulled me away from my most important task. Prayer.

I picked up the phone by Nick's bed and asked if I could please have a Catholic priest come and bless my husband. "Certainly," said the voice on the other end of the line. "We'll send Father Joe."

In the midst of all this, Debbie came in. I told her, "We need to get Nick out of this room. He's so depressed he's giving up. He's going to die!"

We got a Gerry Chair and asked the nurse if she would be kind enough to help us. She agreed and the three of us put Nick in the chair, tubes, IVs and all. We wheeled him down the hall to the sun porch and waited for the priest to come.

When he stepped into the sun porch, he looked toward the wheel chair said, "Nick, I'm Father Joe. Do you want to be blessed?" He was an older man with a nice smile.

Nick could barely lift his head. He looked out of the corner of his eye and said, "Yes," nodding slightly.

Father Joe pulled a beautiful gold cross out of his pocket and explained, "This is a very special cross with healing powers."

After he prayed, he said, "Nick, look at me. I was like you three times. I had a stroke and nearly died. Look at me now. I can do anything. I play racquetball and I ski." I could see my husband gazing steadily into the man's eyes. What the Father was saying was registering! Because of Nick's love of sports, he connected immediately with the priest's words.

Father Joe headed toward the door. I thanked him and he left – so abruptly that I felt abandoned, thinking, "He's gone, but what did he do? He didn't do anything!" What did I want him to do? I wanted a miracle!

All of a sudden, Nick lifted his head. He looked at me and said, "Judy, take me to my room. I want to eat." A miracle had occurred!

When I wheeled Nick into his room, one of his bosses and another friend from work were waiting for us. This was the second time they had driven all the way from Youngstown, Ohio to visit Nick. Immediately they noticed his improvement and rejoiced.

I ordered him a tray of food with breaded pork chops, which he loved, potatoes and Jello. He ate it like it was his last meal instead of the first in a long, long time. We were so excited!

Nick's friend from work said, "I'm going down to Pizza Hut and get him some pizza and pop." Everyone wanted to feed him!

All of a sudden, he said, "Okay, I'm ready to go back to bed now."

Nick was talking and getting stronger moment by moment. There HAD been a miracle! Why should we ever doubt the power and faithfulness of God?

Since the doctor hadn't listened to my pleas against surgery, I prayed, *"God, please make my husband even stronger so he can tell the doctor what he wants."*

For the next couple of nights after the children and I had

visited Nick in the hospital to decorate his room, Lindsey had awakened crying. "Mommy, Daddy is asleep. He doesn't remember anything." Nick had fallen asleep after other seizures and hadn't recognized her. I asked, "Why is this upsetting you so much this time?"

She had wiped her tears and said, "He was supposed to put up our scarecrow." Lindsey loved to decorate. She and her father had begun to put up the scarecrow before he got sick, but they never finished the job. I consoled her the best I could. The next day I reminded Nick of the unfinished task.

One night after I had come home from the hospital and Nick was doing better, the reality of his close call with death overwhelmed me. I phoned him and sobbed, "Nick, you can't die yet. Lindsey and Nicholas need a father, and I'm not ready to let go of you."

He tried to comfort me. "Honey, I'm not going to die yet."

I gave Lindsey the phone. She told him, "Daddy, you have to come home and help me put up the scarecrow."

Late on Tuesday evening, the doctor came to my husband's room. After his visitors politely left the room, the doctor asked, "Nick, how do you feel?"

"I feel great."

"Does your neck hurt?"

"No."

"Are you vomiting any more?"

"No. I feel great. I ate. I even got up and tried to walk. I feel really good."

"Well, Nick, I had you on the schedule for surgery for Thursday. I planned to insert a permanent drain called a shunt."

Nick asked, "What choices do I have? Is there anything else you could do?" I felt like he was echoing me, asking all the appropriate questions. Normally I asked all the technical questions. I was amazed!

The doctor explained, "I can do the surgery, or I can do a CAT scan and see what's going on in there. I can check your pressure, and with this temporary drain, we can check for an infection and for elevated pressure. What do you think?"

Nick said, "I'd like to try the temporary drain again and see what happens."

The next day the doctor did the CAT scan. He came to Nick's room and told us there was no herniation or shift in the brain, so he had inserted the temporary drain. There was no evidence of an infection. His cerebral spinal pressure and the fluid were all normal. His findings confirmed that we had been given a miracle.

As the doctor walked out of the room, our friends who were waiting in the hallway heard him say to the nurse who had accompanied him, "Cancel the surgery."

What? I said to myself. Then he added, "But he is still on for Thursday."

Then he hesitated and came back to the doorway of the room and said, "I canceled it altogether."

Quickly I pulled him back into the hallway. "Doctor, he doesn't need the surgery?"

"No," he said. "He doesn't need surgery any more."

I was elated! "Wow! Do you think he got a miracle? I had him blessed."

"Yes, I do."

"Doctor, are you a religious man?"

"I believe in a higher power, absolutely."

"Then you DO think Nick got a miracle!"

He answered, "Yes."

"Doctor, remember three years ago when you told me it would take a miracle to keep Nick from needing an operation for the scar tissue? Well, we didn't get our miracle then, but we've got it now!"

Nick's roommate who had suggested that I'd better pray had gone home, but I heard that he had been re-admitted to a room a few doors down and was having some problems. I asked about him and a nurse took me to his room. He suffered some vision impairment, so I said, "I'm the wife of Nick Shirilla, your former roommate. Do you remember me?"

"Yes, I do," he said.

"Do you recall when you told me, 'I reckon you should call on the Lord"?

"Yes, I do."

"Well, I want to thank you, because when I was in a most confused state, you showed me the way. I came to tell you that my husband just got a miracle. He was cured."

"Praise the Lord!" he responded. "Now you're going to get all kinds of graces."

"Oh, thank you so much!"

That man was right. That day I had originally gone to the hospital to bring Nick home, so I hadn't taken much money and no extra clothes. The doctor thought it was a good idea for Nick to stay in town one more day after he was discharged, just to make sure he was doing well. Everything I needed was provided for me. It was as though I was wearing a T-shirt that said, "Feel Sorry for Me! My husband has a brain tumor."

Nick's boss's wife arranged for Nick and me to spend the extra day at the Omni Hotel – in a suite! The pharmacy had given me more than one and a half days' supply of medication to get me through the next two days. Everyone was so kind to me. I felt God's graces.

I tried to take Nick to the restaurant, but he got so weak I had to take him back to our room. I ordered a fruit plate, some wings and other munchies

The cleaning lady came, but I told her, "Don't worry about cleaning. This room is so immaculate. Just make the bed." I offered her some of our food.

She was going to sweep, but I told her, "Don't even worry about sweeping.

She brought us extra pillows, chocolates and some ice. After she got the bed ready she asked, "Do you need anything else?"

I thanked her and told her no.

That night while Nick was sitting on the sofa in the hotel room, he asked, "Judy, what's that white piece of paper on the table?"

I thought, *Wow! Even though he's so weak, he doesn't miss a trick!*

I picked it up, thinking it might have been from the doctor. It said, "Hi! I am your cleaning lady. You were so kind to me. So was your husband. I will be praying for Nick that he does well." She signed her name.

Later on she knocked on our door. I invited her in and we chatted for a little while. She had a dear friend who had cancer so she knew what I was going through. I needed to talk to somebody because I was so desperately scared. She gave me hope and pepped me up.

There are so many wonderful people in the world. God's blessings never stop.

The Gift of Time

Nick was like the Energizer bunny. He had nine lives and kept recharging – going and bouncing back. One of the first tasks he undertook when he got home was to finish putting up the scarecrow.

After we'd been home for two weeks, Nick started getting symptomatic again. I talked with a doctor at our local hospital. He said, "They may have to put an elective shunt in to alleviate some of that pressure." I knew once that shunt went in, it was permanent. That meant the end was near. We tried to postpone the surgery as long as possible to give Nick time to heal and get stronger.

By the next to the last week in October we knew we couldn't postpone the inevitable any longer. Nick went back to the Cleveland hospital and a ventricular shunt was inserted. Nick came through the surgery well.

We had a great Halloween and prepared for Thanksgiving and Christmas.

Many times after his surgeries and once after an implant a metal ring had to be put around his head and screws inserted. It was awful to look at. I likened that ring to Jesus' crown of thorns. It was comforting to remember that Jesus suffered for us and knows about our suffering and pain.

Nick felt great throughout November. He decorated, getting ready for Christmas. He was like Kris Kringle!

One day he started to climb a ladder in the garage. He got half way up and I panicked! "Nick! What if you get up there and have a seizure? You'd better come back down!"

I called our neighbor and he climbed up for us.

Soon he started to talk about putting a new roof on the house.

I said, "Aw, That's silly. You're not even working. Besides, we don't need to spend that much money."

"Judy, I WANT to put it on!"

"Well, let's wait until spring."

"Nope!" he persisted. "I might be bad then. I want to see it done."

He must have had a premonition,"I thought, remembering the doctor's warning, "The brutal reality is that Nick will not be here next Christmas." I had always been honest with my husband – very open and honest. I wondered, *Should I tell him? Do I have a right to withhold this information?*

One day, I said, "Nick, there's something the doctor told me about your prognosis. Do you want to know?"

He hesitated. "Well... Yeah."

I told him exactly what the doctor had told me.

"No!" he responded emphatically. "He didn't say that! No sir! What does he know?"

In a way telling Nick turned into a blessing. It gave him time to get his affairs in order.

God was so very good to us! He had given us more time to prepare the children by talking with them about their daddy's condition. Extended time also gave Nick and me the opportunity to point out to them how blessed we were.

One day when I was driving home with Nicholas in the car, I said to him, "Look at your little friend, Nicholas. His daddy left his mom when he was one year old. He never had an opportunity to know his dad. And look at your other friend. His mom and dad are divorced and he doesn't get to spend nearly as much time with his dad as you do. Look at all the things you and your dad have done together. He's taught you how to play basketball. He's watched you play flag football and basketball and baseball. Look at all the fun things you've done together. God could have taken your daddy during his very first surgery, but He keeps giving us more time."

I asked him, "Do you feel cheated, Nicholas?"

"No, Mommy." I was so proud of my brave little boy, and of Lindsey, too. They displayed so much courage for their young age. Their childhood was difficult and traumatic much of the time, but they faced their challenges with optimism and bravery.

Many situations have demonstrated how sensitive they are to the problems of others. Once, when we were at the movies, we were coming out of the restroom area just as a gentleman was pushing a woman in a wheelchair. Nicholas, only seven at the time, quickly held the door. Later he said, "Oh, Mommy, I feel sorry for that lady." He remembered when his dad had to use a wheelchair. Both children show much empathy for other people's problems.

God also gave us more time to spend with Him. During the last three years of Nick's life, we had made such a faith conversion. We had visited Our Lady of Fatima statue while on tour it was presented at Our Lady of Fatima Church in Farrell, Pennsylvania. She is known to have a lot of healing powers. Some people claim to have seen her shed real tears. Others claim they have seen real teeth on her. I reminded Nick, "You know, I'm not the one who is sick. Do you believe in miracles? I do, but you must believe, too."

"Yeah, I do," he said.

Nick said he had seen her smile and had seen two teeth, but I had not. Her face revealed to me the face of my maternal grandmother's face. She had passed away right before Nicholas was born. I thought, *My grandmother would be heartbroken to know how my husband is suffering.* She loved Nick dearly. I knew she must have been watching over us.

Every night before we went to bed, we said the "Our Father," "Hail Mary," and "Glory Be." Then Nick prayed with the children. Nearly every night after they were tucked in bed, he asked, "Judy, did they say their prayers?"

Back in August, Nick had come in the house and said with excitement, "Judy, come with me and see what I bought for Lindsey!"

I got in the car with him and he drove me to a bike shop. As we were getting out of the car, he said to me, "You know I've got to get her a bike for her fifth birthday. I got Nicholas his bike for his fifth birthday."

He pointed to a purple bike with pretty streamers on the handlebars and a cute banana seat. "It'll take her a couple of years to grow into it, but I wanted to get her one that would last a while." He'd ordered black tires instead of the whites so they wouldn't show the dirt and put the bike in layaway until her fifth birthday on November 16. Daddy's little girl still gets much enjoyment riding that bike.

Nick felt so good during the month of November. One day I went shopping with my sister. When we came home, Nick was outside decorating the fence with fresh pine roping. He turned and looked at us as we pulled into the driveway. His face lit up with excitement and happiness. The look on his face that day is a beautiful memory I will always cherish.

The Inevitable

For eight years the fear of Nick having a seizure while driving the car hung like a dark cloud in the back of my mind. The possibility of my husband having the children in the car and getting into an accident enlarged that ominous cloud.

On the morning of December 12, he decided to take Nicholas to breakfast before school because he knew that he would be starting on chemotherapy the following week.

"No, Daddy," Nicholas had told him as he got ready for school. "You go yourself this time."

Nick decided to go mail the Christmas cards, then stop at McDonalds' and bring breakfast home for the three of us.

I made some coffee, lit all the trees and waited for my husband to return. After Nick had been gone for at least 45 minutes, I started feeling panicky, as though something terrible had happened. I began to pace the floor. *Something isn't right! Where is he? Why isn't he home?*

Nicholas came in the room and asked, "Mommy, is Daddy here yet? My bus is going to be coming soon."

"Nicholas, I think something has happened. I'm afraid Daddy's been in an accident. He should have been home by now. I'll make you some Quaker oats so you can eat."

I kept glancing out the window as I put my son's toast in the toaster. I walked into the living room and looked out that window. After I looked up and down the street I turned away and prayed, *God, please why can't I see our van coming? Please let him come home safely.* Again I looked outside. There was a police cruiser in the driveway!

My heart sank to my feet as an awful wave of fear came over me. I couldn't imagine why a policeman was coming to my door unless ... unless Nick had been killed in an accident.

I opened the door. "Mrs. Shirilla?"

"Yes." I could barely respond. Before he could even deliver his message I asked, "Was my husband in an accident?"

"Yes, he was. On route 224 right in front of Monroe Muffler. We were driving behind him. He had a seizure, we could tell. He accelerated, then ran off the road and hit a telephone pole."

The inevitable had occurred. "AHH!" I said. "Is he all right?"

"He's okay. He's in emergency, and doing well. But he didn't have his seat belt on and he hit his head. Your van is totaled."

"Oh, my God! His poor head!"

"I need to come in and ask you some questions." He was a big, broad-shouldered gentleman.

Just as he stepped into the living room, my son ran by and spotted the police uniform. Overcome with fear, he dashed into the bathroom and never came out until the officer left.

During the time the policeman filled out his report, I called to Nicholas several times, but he never answered. I finished answering the policeman's questions and he left.

"Nicholas!" I called one more time. "Come on. Mommy will drive you to school." I called my neighbor to come and stay with Lindsey who was still asleep. Then I phoned my mother-in-law and father-in-law. They headed up to the hospital right away.

Once we were in the car and going down the street, I told my son, "Daddy is okay. After I drop you off at school, I'll go spend some time with him."

As we drove down 224, Nicholas said, "Mommy, Mommy, let's go by and see the pole Daddy hit." The pole was cracked in half, right down the middle.

Two days prior to the accident Nick had a Dilantin level drawn. They liked to keep his level high – at least 12.0 - because he was such a big guy. The morning of the accident, his level was 7.0, probably what had caused the seizure.

Later I drove to the junkyard to see the van. There was a hole in the windshield. I observed that without the seat belt on, he must have been gently thrown off to one side, landing on the seat. My husband was very conscientious about wearing his seat belt. If he forgot, the children always reminded him. I was convinced that if he'd had his seat belt on, he would have died instantly.

When I went back to the hospital to see him, he said, "Judy, at the time of my accident I could feel a soft hand holding my hand. I thought maybe it was you."

"No, that was your guardian angel," I told him.

Nick was anxious to get home from the hospital so he wouldn't miss his 15th annual Christmas party at work. After 15 years of service, an employee was given a big television. Nick was excited about that.

His doctor was not on-call that day, and the doctor covering for him refused to release Nick before he knew his whole case history.

"I am going home regardless," Nick announced. "I'm signing myself out. I'm NOT missing my Christmas party."

When I told the doctor, he asked, "Are you willing to take the responsibility if something happens?"

He firmly responded, "Yes I am." I could understand that Nick probably realized this might be his last Christmas party. Nevertheless I told him that I would not come to pick him up. "I work at the hospital," I reminded him. "You are signing yourself out against medical advice. I'll ask your dad to bring you home.

The party was at a beautiful, fancy restaurant. Nick received his television set. He and I enjoyed that evening with his co-workers.

On Christmas Eve, on our way to my parents' home for dinner, Nick announced, "We have to go through this car lot. I want to look for a van."

I argued, "Nick, we don't need another van right now. You're not working and you're not going to be driving for a while because you'll be starting your treatments."

"No," he argued, "we need to get another van. Besides, when I go back to work, I'll have to have a car to drive." He was born a Taurus, truly a stubborn bull!

We didn't find one Christmas Eve, but the following week he went van hunting with our neighbor who was unemployed at the time. They found a beautiful '90 conversion van, in excellent condition. A dentist had traded it in. And it just happened to be maroon and gray, Ohio State colors.

I remember driving it home from the car lot. "Wow! This is so big! I can't drive this!"

Nick said, "What do you mean you can't drive it? It's only one foot longer than our other one." I did learn to drive it and we still have it today. At the time of this writing it has over 120 thousand miles on it and it's still going. We've taken a lot of trips with that van and experienced a lot of enjoyment. I'm so grateful we bought it.

Several times in January I was awakened because our

bed was shaking vigorously. Nick was having seizures. What a nightmare! He made frequent trips to the bathroom due to some of the medication he was taking.

Early one morning, after a difficult night, he woke up and headed for the bathroom. I didn't want him to feel like I was babying him, but I couldn't help but follow him down the hallway to see if he'd make it okay.

Another time he was unable to sleep, so he went into the living room to watch TV. When I awoke and realized he wasn't in bed, I went to the living room and discovered that he was in the middle of a seizure. He was conscious, but his hand shook involuntarily. His face and his eyes twitched.

I was scared he might lose consciousness and even lack oxygen, so I called 911. They came to check him and he was fine. *Thank God!* I thought. *I don't have to take him to emergency.*

VII.
CLINICAL TRIAL

Don't Quit!

It's funny how you get premonitions. About mid-January, I was sitting in the basement sorting the laundry when all of a sudden a strange feeling came over me. A voice inside whispered, *Spring, spring. Nick is going to be bad.* In my mind I pictured a funeral and people walking by a coffin.

That scared me! On impulse I ran upstairs and said to my husband, "Nick, Nick, honey, do you want to go somewhere? Do you want to go on a little trip now that you are feeling better? We could go anywhere you want to go. Mom has said she would watch the children anytime we wanted her to."

Caught off guard, he said, "Well... I don't know... I really don't want to go anywhere..."

"Are you sure? Think about it."

Later that day he called me into the living room. "Maybe I do want to go somewhere," he said. "I just watched a commercial about the Bahamas. Do you want to go to the Bahamas?"

"Okay!"

He continued, "The ad on TV said they have package deals. We could go for three or four days."

I told him, "Okay, I'll call and get some prices. Then I'll call Mom and see if she wants to watch the children. Maybe we can go."

On January 21, the morning we were to leave for the Bahamas, we awakened to four or five inches of snow. I went outside and shoveled out our driveway, then decided to shovel the neighbor's, since they had been so helpful through all our ups and downs.

I realized I was working off nervous energy. In recent weeks I had worked hard enough to move mountains because of my adrenaline flow. The exercise combined with the cold air felt exhilarating. Near the time for our departure, I filled a little pharmacy bag with all of Nick's medications. Although our family had some apprehensions about the trip, I assured them we would be fine. "They have oxygen on the plane," I told them. "God has assured me that Nick will be okay. This was meant to be."

We left Ohio in freezing weather and arrived for our four days in the Bahamas in 80 degree, sunshiny weather. We loved it! The beaches were beautiful, and so was our room. We enjoyed the pool, the reggae music, the restaurants and the shopping.

Girls kept coming to me to ask, "Can I put a braid in your hair? Can I put a braid in your hair?" Finally I gave in. My husband and I were a colorful pair – me with beads in my braided hair and Nick with a bandanna on his head to protect it from the sun. I had teased the young girl who had adorned my hair. "Why don't you do a braid in my husband's?"

"Really?" she said. "Does he want a braid?"

He laughed and took off his bandanna. She laughed, too, when she saw that he had no hair.

I took lots of pictures. Today I love to get them out and go through them, because my husband looks so happy in them. He was able to stay up late so we could go to the casino. In the daytime we did lots of walking.

One day while strolling through the markets, he told me, "You know, Judy, I can't believe how good I've felt since I've been here. In this warm weather I feel great!"

We stopped at a straw market and bought a straw doll for Lindsey with her name on it. Later we bought Nicholas some bongos and a T-shirt.

Our vacation trip couldn't have been more ideal.

Although Nick continued to suffer from a lot of head-aches, the first couple of weeks in February went well. On President's Day, February 17, Nicholas was up early as usual. Lindsey was our late sleeper. I was reading in the living room.

When our son saw his dad walking down the hallway, he got excited. "Daddy, Daddy, I'm off school today."

"Good," Nick told him. "We'll play. We'll do things." He went on to the bathroom.

A few moments later I heard a loud noise, so loud it sounded like somebody had fallen on our roof. I said to no one in particular, "Oh, my goodness! I wonder what happened?"

As I searched through the rooms, I thought, Maybe *Lindsey rolled out of bed.* I checked, but she was still fast asleep. As I returned to the living room, I noticed the bathroom door was shut. I pushed on the door but it wouldn't open all the way.

I cried out, "Oh, my gosh!" Nick had been thrown off the commode by a seizure. He was

on the floor, his head banging once, twice, three times as though he was doing pushups. "What are you doing?" I asked him.

"Judy, you've got to help me. I went into a seizure and fell on the floor." Once again I tried to open the door without success. His whole body was lodged against it.

I called to our son, "Nicholas, can you help me? Maybe you can squeeze through so we can help your dad." There wasn't enough space for him to get through, so I called 911 for the ambulance drivers had to come and take the hinges off the bathroom door so I could enter. Before they arrived the firemen came and broke the bathroom door and helped Nick get back to his feet, then walked him back to the bed.

One of the men said to Nick, "Why do you look familiar to me?" When I commented that he'd just had an accident in December, he said, "That's why I recognize you. I was at that accident. You know, you always remember the nice ones."

He turned to me and said, "Your husband was so kind!"

I teased Nick, "I guess you made quite an impression!"

Once he was settled back in bed, Nick said, "I'm okay now. There's no need to take me to emergency."

"Fine," one of the attendants said. "But we'll stay here with you for a while." They gave him some oxygen. All he wanted was his remote so he could watch television.

I vaguely remembered our neighbor walking through the house All of a sudden his familiar face became clear in the midst of the sea of faces in our home. "Dom!" I said.

"Is everything okay? May I go see Nick?"

Dom had cancer 20 years before – a tumor behind his nose. He'd become bedridden and unable to eat or drink - a near-death experience. He remembers the day he jumped out of his bed all of a sudden and started doing pushups. He was miraculously healed!

Dom told me that morning, "Judy, Nick keeps telling me he wants to go to Houston, Texas, to see a doctor who is known for research and treatment for brain tumors. You should take him. My parents took me on a bus to Roswell, a cancer institute in Buffalo, New York. Look at me now! I'm doing great!"

"I know," I said. "Ever since he read about that doctor he's been talking about going to see him." I thought to myself, *Okay. God is talking to me through my neighbor. I need to take Nick, even though I am scared to death when he has these frequent violent seizures.* I told Dom, "Okay, I'll take him if this is something he wants to do."

I started making phone calls – first to a cancer institute in Houston, Texas, then to a social worker at our local hospital. She made most of the arrangements for us to go.

Even though Nick had been through six brain surgeries, three of them recurrences, can you believe we still had hope? Faith? Trust? Maybe he WOULD be one of the individuals who would beat the awful cancer battle.

I often read the words on a little card someone gave us. It's called <u>Believe in Miracles</u> by Emily Matthew. It says,

When things have gone wrong, as they sometimes will do,
Or an obstacle suddenly pops into view,
You have got to believe this is merely a stop
And eventually you are bound to come out on top.
So whatever you do, just don't quit!

We are all running a race in life. Sometimes we run very fast and sometimes we drag, wondering if we'll ever reach the finish line. But then we see a glimpse of hope and light at the end of our dark tunnel. If we quit too soon, we'd lose the race of life. We must keep the faith and complete the race, because at the end Jesus waits with His arms wide open to greet us. Exhausted, we fall into His arms! You see, we dare not quit!

Many times Nick became discouraged and said, "Judy, I'm getting tired. What sense is there to continue to fight, to keep going?" Sometimes he'd say, "I'm tired of taking all these pills. I'm just sick of it!"

I'd tell him, "Nick, I can't imagine what this is like for you. In my limited life experience, I can only relate it to having a baby. When I went in to have Nicholas and Lindsey, I had no idea what would happen to me. I was so vulnerable at those times. I went through the process of labor and delivery and all the pain that went with it. A LOT of pain. But what happened? The labor pain subsided and I gave birth to a healthy, beautiful infant. Suddenly the pain was completely forgotten.

"Nick, I know you have suffered a lot as you have battled these recurrences. But ultimately you will be healed, if not on this earth, then in eternal life as God has promised. You must feel like you're going through a dark tunnel, but at the end of your tunnel you will find this awesome, beautiful Person, this ray of light. Jesus will be there to greet you and take you home."

Thoughtfully he said in a somber tone of voice, "It's hard to believe sometimes."

I told him, "No, you MUST believe. You must believe with

your whole heart. Just as I had that beautiful baby to show for my pain, you are going to have eternal life and a crown to show for yours. This is what life is all about. It's the only purpose for life that I can come up with. This is part of the reason why people suffer."

Through those dark days we clung to Psalm 23, the Good Shepherd's poem. It can never be read too often. Will you read it with me now?

The Lord is my Shepherd, I shall not want. He maketh me to lie down in green pastures: he leadeth me beside the still waters. He restoreth my soul: he leadeth me in the paths of righteousness for his name's sake. Yea, though I walk through the valley of the shadow of death, I will fear no evil, for thou art with me; thy rod and thy staff comfort me. Thou preparest a table before me in the presence of my enemies: thou anointest my head with oil; my cup runneth over. Surely goodness and mercy shall follow me all the days of my life and I will dwell in the house of the Lord forever.

I hope reading that brought you comfort and inspiration. Although Nick and I faced many dark days and numerous blocked pathways, we had to persevere. When we did, we always found peace.

Through perseverance and prayer we can overcome the obstacles in our lives and come out ahead. I also remind you once again how important it is to keep your sense of humor. We received an American Greeting Card from the Carlton Collection that has a smiling face on the front of it. It says, *"Sometimes the only sense you can make of life is a sense of humor."* When you open it, you read, *"Keep smiling, at least you have got the right attitude."*

This is so true. Nick reminded me over and over, "Judy, you have to have a sense of humor to survive." He'd tell me, "You need only two things to survive in life."

I'd ask, "What is that?"

"A sense of humor and common sense." I'd like to add "Faith in God." Without that, nothing matters.

Renewed Hope

In February 1994, as Nick's tumor had continued to grow, every available means of treatment had been used. It had seemed the hourglass was running out. Then, suddenly, on the day of Nick's fall, our neighbor had walked in, in the midst of our crisis, and had reminded us, "I was like Nick. I'd used all my options. Then I was taken to Roswell and I was cured."

If you see any glimpse of hope, jump on it.

One week later, on February 24, Nick and I boarded a plane to Houston to meet with the specialist and his associates to get some answers and possibly to be accepted for a clinical trial.

Nick had read about clinical trials. They're not always a cure, but through weeks of documented treatments some people have been cured. Time was running out. What did we have to lose?

I was uneasy about the trip to Houston since he'd had so many recent violent seizures. Before we left our doctor advised, "Make sure you have plenty of Dilantin on board."

While on the plane I observed his every move, his every twitch. But God, being the loving kind God that He is, spared me my worst apprehensions.

In the midst of my tension during the flight, I resorted to a silly senseless coping mechanism. About 10 in the morning the stewardess came into the first class section where we were. Nick was in a wheelchair and very weak. She asked everyone, "May I get you a drink?"

I heard the gentleman sitting in front of us say he would take a Bloody Mary. Nick ordered an orange juice. For some wild reason, I said, "I'll have a Bloody Mary, too." Never in my entire life had I even so much as sipped a Bloody Mary! What was I thinking of?

I took one little sip and shuddered. It was the most awful thing I'd ever tasted in my life! Nick looked at me and laughed. He said, "Why did you order that?"

"I have no idea." I probably thought it would drown my

sorrow and make me feel better. I didn't realize it would make me feel worse.

Just then the stewardess returned. I reached out to her with the nearly full glass in my hand and said, "Excuse me. Do you think I could get rid of this and get an orange juice? This really isn't my style." She took the glass and smiled. Sometimes without thinking we reach for relief in the wrong places.

A buddy of Nick's father, also a big Ohio State fan, lives in Galveston, Texas. He picked us up at the airport. Although we'd never met, I recognized him immediately. As I was wheeling Nick off the plane, my attention was attracted immediately to a gentleman wearing a sweatshirt that said, "OHIO STATE BUCKEYES."

After we introduced ourselves he took over pushing the wheelchair. I felt such relief. To meet someone who could take over in my weak moment meant so much to me! He wheeled Nick out to the car, got our luggage and we were on our way to the cancer clinic - a new journey, a new hope.

We were shown around the city and taken to see the location of the institute, having no idea what we would experience in the days that followed.

On a Thursday morning in February, we met with the institute's chief resident of neurology. After introductions, I gave him the films of all Nick's surgeries and of all his pre and post radiation implants. He smiled at my husband and shook his hand, exhibiting sincere empathy and warmth. Immediately I sensed, *Everything's going to be okay.*

We discussed what clinical trials involve and he briefly reviewed my husband's scans. "Your husband has received an awful lot of radiation. It's difficult to determine how much of what I see is radiation, how much is scar tissue and how much is tumor."

I was a bit deflated by his comment. It sounded as though there were so many things growing in that little compartment called 'Nick Shirlla's brain' that it could be only a matter of time before it would pop. I managed to respond to his comment, "Yes, my husband had 30 external radiation treatments. I believe through the first external beam they delivered somewhere between 3,500 and 4,000 rads." His first implant with the five catheters delivered as much radiation directly to the site of the tumor." We're talking about a LOT of radiation! And to think the second radiation implant contained double doses —13 catheters! But what else could they have done when he had this awful monster growing inside his head? They had to attack it with everything in their power.

Then the doctor said, "Later this afternoon I will spend some time looking at your films, Nick. Then I will meet with the entire group of physicians and we will review your case in depth. After that, I will get back with you regarding whether or not we can prescribe a clinical trial for you."

Another greeting card we received, taken from the Carlton Collection of American Greetings, says, *"In every journey there is growth. In every conflict, there is hope. In every action, there is purpose. In every moment of doubt, remember there is my belief in you."* The doctor at the clinic believed in us.

On Friday when we went back to get the news, Nick and I were taken into a consultation room and were told they had reviewed the films and were going to start Nick on a clinical trial. He and I were excited and hopeful. This had to be the miracle pill, that magic pill we'd been searching for!

A nurse sat down with us and went over the entire regimen - when he would begin and what day he would receive which part of the trial. His treatment consisted of two things: an injection called beta-interferon and a pill called CIS/Retonoic Acid.

There are two interferons, alpha and beta. Patients with multiple sclerosis are given alpha-interferon. In Nick's case, beta-interferon, a chemotherapy injection, was used, hopefully to combat and finally kill whatever was left of the tumor.

All the instructions and medications would be sent to us via mail since we'd agreed to be part of their clinical trial. Although we knew there would be certain side effects and certain things we would have to avoid during this trial time, we were willing to do whatever they prescribed.

During our stay in Houston we stayed with a dear cousin of mine who lives there. She and her husband took us to the Astrodome where we watched the first rodeo we'd ever seen. Never had I seen so many cowboys in one place!

Angels for One Another

During one of our routine checkup visits in Cleveland before the clinical trials began, Nick and I met someone who was battling her own bout with a brain tumor..

I had gone into the restroom and noticed a young woman changing her baby's diaper. The baby was a beautiful little girl with bright blue eyes and lots of long blonde curly ringlets. I thought, *She looks like Goldiilocks!* Her mother looked up at me with a desperate expression on her face.

"Are you waiting to see the doctor?" she asked.

"Yes, we are."

"Are you the patient?"

"No, my husband is."

"My name is Julie. Could I meet your husband?" She explained that she'd been wanting to meet somebody else who was young, had a family, and was also experimenting with treatment for a brain tumor.

"Of course you can meet him," I said. We went back out into the waiting room. Nick and Julie bonded immediately. They had so much in common.

They were only about a year apart in age. Both had the same birthday, May 4. She also had an astrocytoma. She had been diagnosed and had her first surgery when her youngest child, her third daughter, was two weeks old.

Nick told her, "My son was two weeks old when I went for my first brain surgery."

She asked, "Nick, where is your brain tumor located?

Toward the end of February, Julie called to tell us her husband would soon be participating in a bowling tournament in Cleveland, Ohio. Since they lived only five hours from Cleveland they would be driving up. After the tournament, they wanted to come to Boardman to meet with Nick and me and take us to dinner.

I told her, "That would be great!"

She said, "Judy, an elderly man I know is going to give me a special traveling rosary to pray for healing. I'm going to bring it so Nick can wear it while we say prayers for him. I know things aren't going well for him right now."

When the four of us got together, I couldn't help but chuckle. Julie talks as much as I do, if not more! The guys talked mostly about sports.

Of course, after a while Julie and I wondered off to the restroom. We were so busy talking that we didn't realize 20 minutes or more had passed by. Suddenly we heard a knock on the door and Nick's voice calling, "What are you girls doing in there?"

I said to Julie, "I guess he and Paul ran out of things to talk about. We'd better go out and rescue them."

After a lovely dinner the four of us went to our house. Julie put the rosary on Nick and the four of us said some very special prayers together.

God always does send us the right people into our lives when we need them the most. That evening, Julie told me, "When I met you I was not dealing well with my situation. I did not have a positive attitude. Instead, I had a lot of anger, because of the way my first surgery had gone. I was very frustrated and desperately needed to talk to somebody who would understand. ...Judy, I believe that day we met in the restroom we sort of became angels for one another."

On occasion Julie complimented Nick and me on how well we were coping with our difficult situation. It meant a lot to her to see our strength and our positive attitude. I like to think we gave Julie hope and that hope began to blossom because of our friendship.

Julie is doing well. At the time of this writing, she has gone past her five-year landmark and remains tumor-free. She is experiencing the richness of life despite the constant unavoidable underlying fear. Often she says, "I want to do

this. I want to be there for my girls, to see them grow up."
She is an inspiration to my family and me, an angel for
us. I do hope I have given her back the same kind of encouragement and inspiration. We will always be friends because
we have so much in common.

Another card from the Carlton Collection reads like this:
*"The more I believe in angels, the more I see them all around
me, in friends, in family and acquaintances. It is amazing
how much goodness you can see, if only you believe. You
are such a special person. I can almost see your wings."*
The wife of Nick's father's friend who met us at the airport in Texas was a cancer patient herself. She had been
treated at the institute and was in remission. She often shares
her story of hope with others. I remind every person who
has battled cancer and is in remission and every family member and everyone who has survived the battle: "Don't remain silent. Don't sit back and think your work is done. We
must all get out there and encourage others. We must become messengers to one another, ambassadors who deliver
strength, hope and belief."

VIII.
FINAL PHASES

NO "No Express Team"

Nick began the clinical trials March 2. On March 6, he became very sick and suffered another seizure. His blood pressure shot up. He was so restless!

I called the ambulance and he was admitted to the Intensive Care Unit for a few days. I spent a good part of that first night at the hospital. In the wee hours of the morning, the medication began to take hold and Nick was finally resting. The nurse said, "Why don't you go home and get a little rest?"

I agreed with her, because I wanted to be home to get the children ready for school.

Soon after Nicholas boarded the bus, just before the time to get Lindsey ready for preschool, the social worker from the hospital called. "Hi, Judy! This is Cindy. How are you?"

"I'm okay."

"Judy, I think you'd better come up to the hospital. Things aren't going very well."

"Cindy! Is he still alive?"

"Yes, but he's not doing well. I think you should come up."

"I'll be right there!" I jumped up from the chair and quickly phoned my mother to come stay with Lindsey, then went into my daughter's bedroom. She was already awake and playing with her toys. She was my little angel.

Many times during tense days I thanked God for Lindsey. I looked at her and remembered Nick's words: "If we're going to have another child, we should have one now." I thought, *God gave us this little angel to help us through.* Her wisdom, her insight and cheerfulness often astounded us.

I began to sob. "Lindsey, Daddy is very sick. The hospital just called and I must go up there. Do you think he's okay?" Here I am, asking a five-year-child what she thinks!

She put her brightly colored clown blanket around her like a cape, like the cape of an angel. I walked out of the room and she closed the door. Before I ever walked away, I heard musical sounds and opened the door again.

My little angel daughter was singing the familiar Christmas song, "Gloria in Excelsius Deo." She looked up at me with her beautiful hazel eyes. I repeated, "Lindsey, is Daddy going to be all right?" I NEEDED reassurance!

Her response sounded like a voice from heaven. "Daddy is going to be all right, Mommy." My strength was renewed.

My sister Jan went with me to the hospital. A doctor was waiting for us in the hallway. As I walked down the corridor, he said in an intense tone of voice, "Are you Mrs. Shirilla?"

"Yes, I am." I feared what I would hear him say next.

"I need to talk with you right away about making your husband a no express team."

"No express team" means there would be no cardiac pulmonary resuscitation (CPR) done to revive Nick in the event of a respiratory or cardiac arrest. He wouldn't be put on a ventilator and no medication could be given.

"Pardon me?" I looked around, shaking like an earthquake inside. Cindy, the social worker, was standing off to one side.

"I need to talk with you about making Nick a no express team." Fortunately, less than a month before, Nick and I'd had the foresight to discuss this. We had talked about Powers of Attorney and Living Wills. I had said to him, "Nick, they would like you to sign a living will to become part of your chart. It will give your doctor some idea of what your wishes are. Let me explain to you what it means."

He had said, "I want everything done to keep me alive. Everything."

"I know you do. But in the event you can no longer walk

or talk or eat and you are in a terminal state, do you still want everything done?"

"Well...maybe not at that point. But anything short of that, yes."

The doctor pointed his finger in my face and said, "Mrs. Shirilla, your husband is very bad. He's having some terrible, terrible seizures and we don't know what we should do. Do you want us to make him a no express team?"

I shuddered at his directness, but managed to say to him, "No to the no express team status. These are my husband's wishes. I just had him to a cancer institute last week. He's just begun clinical trials. He is hopeful and wants everything in your power done until you deem it inevitable that he will not recover."

He stared at me, making sure he'd heard my instructions clearly. "Okay," he said. "Then I will transfer him to the Unit."

I thought, "My goodness! They were going to deny my husband care in the Intensive Care Unit!" Then I asked, "Doctor, has my husband had his Dilantin and Decadron this morning? Decadron is an important drug. It keeps the swelling down and prevents violent seizures."

Just then Nick's nurse walked by. The doctor checked with her and she said, "No he didn't receive his Decadron this morning. He couldn't swallow it."

By this time I felt extremely defensive so I said, "Not to be smart or anything, but could they give it to him intravenously? It's so important that he gets this. I'm sure it would help his present condition."

The doctor said, "Okay, we'll give it to him by IV." He also saw to it that Nick received his Dilantin intravenously.

While Nick was being transferred to the Intensive Care Unit, I began to make lots of phone calls. My first call was to my Parish. My connection with the church has been a main source of comfort and strength all my life. I became a member of this particular church 10 years ago, right after Lindsey was born. She was baptized there.

I asked to speak with a priest and Father John came to the phone.

"Father, my name is Judy Shirilla. I'm a member of your Parish and so is my husband, Nick. Could you possibly visit my husband today in the Intensive Care Unit? He has a brain tumor and there has been a significant change for the worse in his condition."

"Yes, I can come." It wasn't long until he arrived in the very small waiting room of the Intensive Care Unit, already filled with Nick's co-workers, neighbors, family and friends. Together, we prayed for God's will to be done. Prayer is so powerful. Father then went into Nick's room with me. He blessed Nick, then we prayed and prayed again.

Jan had shared with me many times that during Nick's eight years of illness, she had prayed, "God, as long as my brother-in-law lives, would You please grant him a good quality of life?" God must have heard her prayers.

Because of my profession as a nurse, I have learned that the quality of a patient's life should be our first concern. I'm always checking to see. What I can do to strengthen this patient's quality of life? What can I do to make a difference? As the wife of a brain tumor patient I often asked myself, What could I do to make a difference for him, to give life new meaning and new hope? Even after all hope is gone, we must continue to be positive and hopeful, because we still have a quality of life to maintain. Even in the absence of our loved one, we have an obligation to continue to live life to the fullest.

Nick was on the prayer lists and prayer chains of many churches, Catholic and non-Catholic. I believe as God heard my husband's name over and over, our prayers were answered again and again.

I will never forget the conduct of our little seven-year-old gentleman Nicholas. He escorted all our friends and family to and from Nick's hospital room. He was so proud to do this for his daddy. "Come and see my daddy," he'd say. "Here's his room. He's very sick."

I sensed he'd found a purpose which gave meaning to all he was facing in his young life. God was calling him to take over, to be the little man of our family and to be supportive to his mom and dad, his sister and grandparents and friends. His strength shined through the darkness of the moment.

Nick finally was discharged after 11 trying days in the hospital. Although he regained much of the strength on his right side, his left side was nearly paralyzed. He had little use of his arm and had to drag his leg to walk.

New arrangements had to be made. Nick was still fully an express team status, so the need arose for hospice to become involved in his care.

As medical professionals and as family we must always honor the wishes of the patient to the best of our ability.

I was encouraged by reading a book called <u>Pain Is Inevitable: Misery is Optional: Go Stick A Geranium In Your Hat and Be Happy</u> by Barbara Johnson. Barbara went through many tragedies, but her attitude was like Nick's. She suffered the loss of three sons. How does one deal with such tragedy? How does one cope? You must get on with making the most of the part of life that remains. I know from my own personal experience, without faith in God, without love and support and determination, one cannot survive.

Dad often reminded me, "Judy, when you were a little girl learning to ride your bicycle, you would hop on and start riding, fall down, hop on and fall down. You always picked yourself back up again and tried again, determined to learn to ride that bicycle." Only after many falls, bumps and bruises did I learn to ride. That same determination was helping me go through life's hardships.

Many times my dad or mom would comment that I was so strong. I could never take credit for any compliment like that. I must always defer to God who gave me the strength. He comes to the weak and makes them strong. He carries our load. I believe that when our gas tanks are empty, He keeps refueling us if we remain open to His message, His love and His word.

"No express team" would not have been an option for my maternal grandmother, a source of inspiration for me from the time I was a little girl.

At the age of 16, carrying a big trunk of belongings, she came by boat from Poland to a strange new country called the United States and resided for a time in Chicago, Illinois. There she found work and a new life.

When I was a little girl I loved to sit beside her and listen to her tell stories about the "old country" and about her life in the USA. By her first husband, Philip, she bore three children, and lost several by miscarriages. After he died, my grandmother struggled and suffered through the years of The Great Depression.

I never detected anger in her voice. I never heard remorse or regret. She talked a lot about God and His faithfulness and carried her rosary beads wherever she went. After she moved to Youngstown, Ohio, she belonged to St. Cashmere Church. I'll never forget when I was very small, she and my aunt took me to a shrine in Carey, Ohio, called "Our Lady of Consolation, Comforter of the Afflicted."

Not once, but twice she lost a husband. My mother's father died when my mom was 19. He had come into the house after working in the yard and had suffered a massive heart attack. Although the two daughters and one son from her previous marriage were older, again she had to go out and find work to provide for her three small children.

She lost her son. As a young adult, my uncle suffered a heart attack. She watched him struggle on a respirator for several weeks. I witnessed her crying, "Why? Why?" I also witnessed her faithfulness. She was my inspiration.

She lost a grandson. My aunt's second to the oldest son, my godfather, died of a brain tumor after a ten-year illness.

She lost a great grandson. My sister's firstborn died six days after birth. The losses and the love goes on and on.

We love and we lose, but what we stand to gain from how we continue on is a legacy we leave for our children and grandchildren. Hopefully we will make a positive difference in their lives. I never saw my grandmother give up. Many times I heard her say, "What am I going to do?" but she always continued on, praying for more strength in order to endure.

With her as my role model I continued on in my difficult journey.

Funny, But Not Fun

Shortly before Nick began his clinical trials, he was having memory problems. Part of his brain would tell him one thing while another part would tell him something else.

One evening in the latter part of February, Jan had asked, "Could I come over and see Nick before we leave on our trip?" Her husband Jack had to go on a short business trip to Vermont and she was going to accompany him.

I said, "Sure, come on over." By the time she arrived, I'd already put the children to bed and Nick was sitting on our bed.

"Hi, Nick," she said when she walked into his room.

He glanced up and said, "Oh, hi, Debbie." Then he said, "No, you're not Debbie. Hi, Jackie. No, you're not Jackie … Oh, I don't know…"

Nick was always joking, so sometimes we weren't sure if he was being funny or if he was serious. This time, I sensed that he was disoriented.

Nick loved tennis shoes. He had a pair of tennis shoes for every sporting event, be it racquetball, basketball or golfing. Early in our marriage, I had teased him, "I'm working to support your tennis shoe habit." He always kept his tennis shoes spotlessly clean.

That year I bought each of the children a new pair. One day they wore them outside and got them muddy. I told Nick, "The kids got their new tennis shoes dirty."

He said, "That's okay. You set them aside and I'll wash them tomorrow. I'll put them outside to dry in the sun when I go to work." Then he looked at me and said, "Oh, I'm not even working any more, am I?"

Neurological changes can be very subtle or significantly dramatic – change in the level of consciousness, change in breathing, weakness in the extremities. He continued to have violent seizures and memory problems through the first part of March. One day our neighbor called and said, "Nick is so funny. When I went up to the hospital to see him, he said, 'Cathy, how did I get here? Did Judy bring me on a flatbed or a cart?'"

Through all his confusion I began to see the humor in hard times that Nick had often wanted me to claim. One night while he was in the hospital, he asked me, "Judy, are we going bowling or are we going to Cleveland?"

Our trips to Cleveland for treatments, to Pittsburgh for second opinions, to local hospitals, to the Bahamas, to Texas and Columbus, Ohio - all these messages had become so jumbled I had to laugh. I guess my last coping mechanism was to laugh at life. It kept me going. If there's nothing else left to do, we can laugh.

My mother-in-law told me that one day while she was standing at his bedside, he said to her, "Come on over here and give me a big hug." He thought his mother was me.

God gave us an amazing gift, even through the final weeks of my husband's life. Even in the midst of experiencing confusion, Nick never forgot he had a wife and two children. When his mom was with him in the hospital, he would pick up the phone and tell her, "I want to call Judy. I want to check on Nicholas and Lindsey." That much of his memory never was tainted or twisted or tampered with.

After he came home from the hospital the second week in March, he was restless. Many nights he would wake up and talk to me. I enjoyed listening to him. "Who are those people at my doorway?" he asked one night.

"What people?" I asked. "I don't see any people."

"Oh, those ladies in white."

"You see some ladies in white?"

"Yes, I wonder if they have the same kind of problem I have." He waved his hands in the air.

Testing his awareness, I asked, "What do you have, Nick?"

"A brain tumor." I wondered if those ladies he saw were angels.

Nick still managed to walk into the kitchen and sit at the table. One day he cleaned up every morsel of food on his plate then began to eat all the food on my plate.

Decadron makes a person very hungry, so I could get him to eat just about anything in these periods of confusion – things he would have never touched in his normal state.

My aunt made him beef stew. He had difficulty swallowing it, so I had to puree it in the blender. By that time, he had to be spoon-fed. He ate it all, although it was something he never would have eaten before.

The social worker at the hospital was watching him eat one day "He is eating so well," she commented. "This is unbelievable for a cancer patient."

I looked up at her, grinned and said, "Well, think about it – the cancer is not in his stomach, it's in his brain, so the tumor isn't affecting his appetite." We had a good laugh.

Soon he went through a period of vomiting profusely after he ate. I think the tumor was shifting, creating pressure in his head.

Fluctuating blood pressure also had an affect on his overall condition.

St. Patrick's Day was a bad day for Nick. He received a couple of beautiful St. Patrick's Day floral arrangements. The one planter decorated in gold, from one of his dad's friends, was filled with Leprechauns and shamrocks and balloons.

Up until then he'd continued to be vane enough to try to remain independent. I remember one day, he had been walking down our hallway, insisting on maintaining his independence as he dragged that left leg. I had tried to help him, but he'd said, "I can do this myself."

I'd allowed him to be as independent as possible without causing harm. But at one point, I had scolded, "Nick, you're six foot tall and weigh 190 some pounds. If you fall, you're going to fall hard, and I'm not going to be able to pick you up. I'll have to call the fire department or somebody."

He'd given in and let me hold his arm.

But suddenly on this particular day, his legs would no longer perform the function of walking. He stopped abruptly and stood still. My sister Debbie and I rushed to get a chair from the dining room. As we eased him down on the chair, we looked at each other with grief. That was one of the most devastating days of my life!

I had to call my father-in-law and my neighbor to get the wheelchair from the garage and push him into the bedroom.

We had to move our king-sized bed against the wall and Nick's father had to lift his son into the bed. I will always remember that tragic sight. What a bitter, sad moment in time for all of us! Every time I think of that St. Patrick's Day event, I can hear the words of that familiar song, "He Ain't Heavy, He's My Brother."

If a person hadn't known better, he or she could have glanced at my athletic-looking husband and concluded, "Why, he's healthy!"

After Nick fell asleep, I sent everybody home, assuring them, "He's doing okay. I'll probably have a good night." Debbie promised to return later. For several weeks she had been sleeping at our home.

Around 11:30 or 12:00 that night, Nick awoke and said to me, "Mr. ... was just here." This man, then deceased, was my parents' good friend and neighbor.

I said, "He was?"

"Yes, he was here. I was talking to him."

"What did you talk about?" He said my old neighbor talked about his children and updated Nick on what they were doing at the present time.

One of the things he missed the most after he could no longer walk was taking showers. He loved to relax in the shower for 30 minutes before he'd ever begin to wash his hair. After he could no longer walk down the stairs to his

"Buckeye Bathroom," I took him to his parents' house a couple of times to use their walk-in shower.

My father then installed a massage shower hose in our main floor bathroom and we put a shower chair in the tub.

By this time, though, he was unable to use that. I decided I wanted him to have one last shower.

When the orderly from Hospice came, I asked, "Could we please get Nick in the shower?" He could barely fit Nick's wheelchair through our bathroom door. As my husband sat on the chair in the tub he leaned so much I could hardly hold him up.

It was a chore, but between the two of us, we accomplished the task. By the time we dressed Nick and sat him in a chair, we were both exhausted. The orderly looked at me and said, "That wasn't very realistic."

"I know," I told him, "but thank you. You don't know how much it meant to me to give Nick that gift. And you don't know what that meant to him. I know we'll probably never be able to do that again, but I do thank you for your cooperation."

He warned, "One of two things will happen. Either he will get better and we can continue as we have been doing, or he will get worse and we'll have to give him bed baths."

I told him, "That's fine." But he did get that final shower. It was a good feeling.

Each day during the 11 days he was home, he lost more functions - first, the walking, then the talking, then movement all together. He'd stay in that bed until some of us could physically pick him up and assist him. Each day I felt like I was losing another part of my spouse.

In the middle of the night on Friday, March 17 – St. Patrick's Day, Nick became very restless. He woke up and said, "I feel as though I'm going to choke to death!" I had to sit him up and hit him on the back. He became extremely confused as he thrashed in his bed.

I concluded that the tumor was growing and moving along the base of the brain. The brain stem controls your breathing and body temperature. It would be only a matter of time before his ability to breathe would be compressed.

Early Monday morning, when he awakened, I helped him get washed and shaved and put his cologne on. My husband loved to be clean and dressed! Debbie was making his breakfast. We planned to give him breakfast in bed. I turned on TV for him. Doctor Schuller was preaching.

Nick looked up at me from his sitting position and said, "Judy." He put up his index finger. "Here is God and here you are."

I said, "Where are you?"

"Here I am and here is Nicholas and Lindsey and there are the Pearly Gates."

When I heard him mention "Pearly Gates," I asked him, "Nick, do you see the light yet?"

"No. ... Judy, I love you."

"I love you, too, Nick."

Then he said, "I love you ... until death do us part. And that will probably be next week." He was preparing me! He was letting me know!

He spent a large part of the day resting in a deep, lethargic state.

The weeks while Debbie stayed with us, she often said, "Judy, I can't believe the people coming in and out of your house! It's like a revolving door! Don't you get tired of all these people?"

I always answered, "No. I love people, and so does Nick."

That day, Jerry our wonderful Baptist neighbor came over. "Judy," he asked nervously, "may I come in and see Nick?" He promised, "I'll just be a few minutes."

When you live your life with lots of people around, you die surrounded with people. They needed to see him and he needed to see them.

"Sure," I told him. "Come on in." My dad was there, but said he was going to leave for a little bit and take Nicholas for a ride.

Jerry and I walked into the living room where Nick was. He took a little black book from his pocket and said, "Nick, could I pray with you?"

Nick, so weak, so very weak, - almost lethargic – was barely able to lift his head. He managed to look over at his friend and say, "Yes."

Jerry then asked, "Nick, has anybody talked to you about heaven?"

Nick answered, "No."

I got excited and told our friend, "I like this!" He read scripture from his little book, explaining that he'd received it as a gift when he was a young boy. He continued, "Nick, I'm not saying that you're going to die, but, Buddy, you're getting tired. You've been through a long illness and I know you're weary. You've been fighting for a long time. But, Nick, do you believe in heaven?"

"Yes," my husband managed to say.

"Do you want to go to heaven?"

"Yes."

"Buddy, I want to see you there when I die." I'd noticed that Nick had been making a spiritual transformation for several months, praying more with the children each night and talking about God and praying to Him more often. But in the moment that followed our neighbor's words, my husband accepted the Lord Jesus as his Savior.

Go With the Flow

That evening, Nick began to thrash violently again. I called for the ambulance. When they arrived, they checked his blood pressure. It had soared to 200/120, dangerously close to stroking stage. The tumor was affecting vital areas in the brain. Nick was perspiring he was so hot. I had to accept the fact that we were facing the final phase of his terminal illness.

The next morning, I told the doctor that I was ready to make my husband a no express team according to his wishes. Immediately the orders were changed. The only medication administered was anything that would alleviate his symptoms and make him comfortable – Inderal for the blood pressure, Valium and his Decadron. My mother and sister came into his hospital room carrying donuts and coffee. Evidently he'd slept off his Valium. At the sound of their voices, he opened his eyes and said, "Good morning."

My sister asked him, "Nick, do you know what today is?"

He said, "Yes, it's Judy's birthday. Happy birthday, Honey."

He remembered my birthday! What a beautiful gift! But... On my thirty fifth birthday, my husband lay in the hospital, dying. We dare not look at life in terms of thinking we have a right to always get what we deserve. Life is life.

As Nick's condition became worse, I wanted desperately to know what was going to happen next. Was he going to go into a coma? Was he going to have more violent seizures? I called his doctor in Houston and told him Nick's condition.

He said, "Judy, at this time we should stop the clinical trials. They're no longer doing what we hoped they would do. If Nick's head is drooping more, and he's become as weak as you say, he's no longer responding to the medication. The disease is very advanced."

Only a few short weeks ago, my husband and I had been in Houston, sharing hope for a new treatment, a cure, or at least remission. Now I had to face the fact that his disease was so advanced that the treatments must be stopped.

One night, unable to sleep, I phoned the hospital and asked to talk with the resident who had assisted the surgeon. I told him, "Please be honest with me. What is going to happen to Nick? What can I expect? He's having violent seizures. What course is his illness going to take?"

"Judy, Nick has a progressive disease. You can expect one of several things. Either he will begin to seize more frequently and more violently or go into a coma for several weeks prior to dying."

My dad had won a four-day trip to Cancun at work. Mom and Dad had reared four children and rarely had opportunity to travel. They didn't know whether to leave or not. I encouraged them to go. Mom told her son-in-law, "Nick, you'd better hang in there now. You can't die while I'm away."

He did hang in. In fact, on March 22, he was able to come home. I knew he hated being in the hospital and hated hospital food. I wanted him to be home, too, with our children, friends and family. We needed each other's warmth and love.

Up until that time I was blessed to have been able to sleep in the same bed with my husband and still share what was left of the intimacy of our marriage. But when he came home, I had to arrange to have a hospital bed for him. Watching his deterioration and debilitation was difficult. Giving up that intimacy we loved made life even more difficult.

But you go with the flow. Change is bound to happen. Nick's was an uneven flow – high and low times. His life was fading away.

The children and I anxiously awaited his trip home from the hospital by ambulette. We greeted him with open arms and hearts. My son had the chicken pox, which allowed him to miss school, but spend quality time with his dad.

Nicholas and Lindsey amazed me. While their father still could walk, they had helped him around. They had taped a baseball cap on our son's bedroom door and placed a chair in the room for daddy to sit on so he could participate in their game. Nicholas would run out and tell me, "Daddy made 20 out of 25 baskets in my baseball hat!" They were both creative as they continued to go with the flow, keeping Nick going, helping him maintain quality of life.

When their daddy had to spend more time in bed, Lindsey took her stuffed animals into his room to be near him as she played.

She'd ask, "How many animals do I have, Daddy?" or "How many fingers am I holding up?" She realized that Daddy was only able to hold up two fingers at a time, so she made certain the correct answer was always two. He could make the peace sign.

She'd hold two animals behind her back and ask, "How many do I have now?" When Nick would hold up the same two fingers, she'd exclaim, "You win again!"

Often she stood by his bed and read stories to him. Both

of our children had learned how to make the best out of a tragic situation.

As I said before, our yesterdays are past; tomorrow is the future; today is the present. Each day, my children had a present – their dad. I had that gift, too. He never forgot us, no matter how sick he became.

In the course of his final days, Nick developed a relationship with his children and me that was so unique we will treasure it forever.

Hope and Love in Dark Times

Near the end of March, we knew our time together would be limited. Those were days of sadness and weariness – days filled with trials and grief. But we kept our hope. Oh, the art of hope! A well-known maxim states, "Where there is life, there is hope." I like it better when it is reversed: "Where there is hope, there is life."

Hope comes first. Life follows. Hope gives power to life, arouses life to continue to expand, reach out and go on. Hope is the shield and buckler against defeat. It never encourages defeat, but wrestles untiringly with the impossible. It conquers the highest mountain. No situation is hopeless.

Even in Nick's final days we had to remain hopeful – hopeful that Nick was comfortable, hopeful that we could provide him with sufficient love until the end, hopeful that we could alleviate his pain and make his life as rich and full as possible.

Our local newspaper, the Youngstown Vindicator, printed an article entitled "What Cancer Cannot Do." It said, *"Cancer is so limited. It cannot cripple love. It cannot shatter hope. It cannot corrode faith. It cannot destroy peace. It cannot kill friendship. It cannot suppress memories. It cannot silence courage. It cannot invade the soul. It cannot steal eternal life. It cannot conquer the Spirit."*

How true that was in the final days of Nick's life! We continued to share much hope. He still was surrounded with an abundance of love.

My favorite portion of scripture is found in I Corinthians,

chapters 12 and 13. It was read at our wedding and I planned to have it read at Nick's funeral. *"Be ambitious for the higher gifts and I will show you a way that is better than any. If I have the eloquence of men, but I do not have love, I am nothing. I am simply a gong clanging or cymbal clashing. Love is always patient and kind. It is never jealous. Love is never boastful or conceited. It is never rude or selfish. Love does not take offense, and it is never resentful. Love takes no pleasure in other people's sins, but delights in the truth. Love is always ready to excuse, to trust, to hope and to endure whatever comes. Love does not come to an end."*

Even though Nick's life was about to come to a sad ending, hope did not end, and neither did love.

During those final days, Nick's mother often came to spend the night and help during the day so I could get some rest. One evening, while she and I were in the bedroom with Nick, he looked up into my eyes, then into his mother's and said, "Oh, it's so dark. I feel so alone. And I feel so bad when I look at you or my mother."

I think he was trying to leave, but was having a hard time. He had to part, but he had to be ready. Our faith could never have been stronger. Friends continued to come and go like a revolving door. Memories were cherished and talked about and held close to our hearts. Courage was always present, invading our souls. As the cancer increased, our souls strengthened.

Back when Nick was still able to talk, my sister had asked him, "How do you do it? You never complain. You just keep on smiling."

He'd replied, "What good would it do to complain?"

That makes a lot of sense. Complaining wastes a lot of energy. Giving of ourselves and doing something positive sustains us and our loved ones.

If we can help our children build their self-esteem and provide the necessary tools to persevere and endure with a smile, we lay a firm foundation for them. Nick laid that kind of foundation.

He sowed the seed, so to speak, and now we reap. His positive attitude, his smile, his joy and kindness were the foundation. I continue to nurture what he sowed. We all reap.

Another special Bible verse is found in I Thessalonians 5:15. *"See that no one renders evil for evil to anyone, but always try to be kind to each other and to everyone else."*

Kindness isn't hard, nor does it require a special skill. It doesn't take enormous energy to demonstrate kindness. It was something Nick was able to do in his short life on earth.

Friends and neighbors, co-workers and family alike came to spend quality time with Nick. I videotaped each and every visitor. Jan and Jack and their children came often. Nick loved seeing their children as they jumped up on his bed.

Since Nick had no brothers, my brothers-in-law were his buddies. They had become his brothers and they had a hard time parting with him.

On Tuesday, March 28, he was most alert. I wondered if his alertness wasn't the proverbial calm before the storm.

Ted, our neighbor from across the street, came to see him. How we appreciated Ted, who always came when we needed his help.

I asked Nick, "Do you remember what we've always called on Ted to do?"

"Yeah," he said, "Get the birds out of our house."

Before we put a screen on our chimney, birds would get in the house and fly around. This scared Nick and he'd run out the door. We'd call Ted.

Nick's boss and others came that day.

On Wednesday, March 29, he had a quiet, peaceful day – in and out of consciousness, not saying much at all. That evening, around 9:00, the phone rang. It was Rick, Nick's life-long friend who had moved to St. Augustine, Florida. From the time Nick was a small child, Rick had been his neighbor and friend.

"I just got in town," he said. "Is it okay if I come by?"

"Certainly!" I told him.

When he arrived, he walked in Nick's room and called

in his Florida drawl, "Hey, Nick!"

Although Rick wasn't the sports enthusiast Nick was, he headed right to the television and turned it on to a basketball game, then went over by Nick's bed. "Hey, Nick. The game is on"

Nick struggled to open his eyes - the first time he'd opened them that whole day.

My sister asked, "Nick, do you know who's here?"

He said, "Yeah, Rick." How amazing that he could still recognize people!

The two friends had shared a lot of good memory making times together when they were small. Rick talked about how they had learned to tie their shoes together, walked to school together, about all the cookouts they'd had in the back yard. His trip to Ohio to see his old friend meant a lot to us.

That night, Nick's cousin, an orderly, offered to spend the night. He sat up all night so I could sleep.

IX.
DEATH COMES

Final Hours

Early Thursday morning, Nick's cousin came in and woke me. "Judy, I think Nick is having a seizure."

I jumped off the couch where I was sleeping and ran into the bedroom. He WAS having a seizure! Quickly I got his Decadron and Dilantin ready, then waited. After he calmed down, I phoned his nurse and asked if we could give him his medication by a different route. While waiting for her to call back, I talked with Debbie. She said, "If he's more alert now, and able to swallow, go ahead and give them to him. But if he's having difficulty swallowing, rub on his throat."

That is what I did and it managed to help him to get his pills down, mixing some of them with applesauce. Knowing that he had his medications in him made me feel better.

Something felt different about that day. About 10:00 a.m., Nick's father brought his mother over on his way to work and stayed a while. About 45 minutes later, Nick became congested and developed a rattle in his chest. He coughed, looked at me and said, "I love you."

I remembered the Bible verse in I Corinthians, *"Love does not come to an end."*

Our children spent a lot of time near Nick, gently climbing in and out of their daddy's hospital bed. After the Hospice people arrived, our bedroom filled up with equipment. They brought a portable x-ray machine and pumps. Soon it began to look like a hospital room.

This is not right! I thought. *This is not supposed to happen! Our bedroom isn't supposed to look like this!*

108

Sue, the nurse, reminded me to give Nick his medication later that evening. I became excited and said, "I don't think I can do that right now. I don't think I can be his nurse anymore. I just want to be with him as his wife."

She said, "No problem. I'll send a nurse back tonight at 10 p.m."

After Sue left I felt totally alone. I became extremely angry. All of a sudden the grim reality that Nick was dying surfaced. I banged my hands so hard on the side rail of the hospital bed; it felt as though I had broken bones in both of my pinkie fingers. "Here I am, a nurse," I lamented, "and often able to help support and sustain the lives of others, but I can do absolutely nothing to save my husband's life!" I felt so out of control, so helpless!

My mom walked in in the midst of my sobbing. "Why, why, WHY does he have to die?" I asked her. "He's so good! Why does he have to die?"

I didn't want to let go. Letting go of someone you love is painfully difficult

One Sunday our pastor had included in our church bulletin a beautiful story about letting go. It was about a little girl named Jenny who had saved her hard-earned money to purchase an inexpensive string of imitation pearls. She cherished them and wore them all the time.

One night, her daddy came into her room and asked, "Jenny, can I have those pearls?"

"No, Daddy," she replied. "Not my pearls! You can have my Beanie Babies or my dolly, but not my pearls!"

Her father said, "Okay, Jennie."

The next night the father returned to her room and asked again, "Jenny, can I have your pearls?"

"No, Daddy, not my pearls. Anything but my pearls."

Finally, after many nights of being asked the same question, Jenny went into her father's room and said, "Daddy, I really love you. I want you to have my pearls."

He took the pearls and thanked her. Then he pulled out of a box a beautiful necklace of authentic precious pearls and put it around Jenny's neck.

How helpful that message was! I learned the more I let go of my precious pearl, the more God could take over.

What are you clenching to so tightly that you don't want to let go? Only through the grace and strength of God could we let go of the one we loved.

About noon, the doorbell rang. I opened the door and there stood a gentleman I had never seen before. He introduced himself and said, "I work with Nick. May I come in?"

His presence caused an unidentified discomfort with me. I had never heard Nick talk about anyone with that name. I told him that Nick was very bad and he understood.

Someone in our crowd of people suggested later, "Did you ever think that was death calling?"

I said, "No."

She added, "I've heard that death calls like that." Perhaps he was "death calling," but I learned later that he really did work with Nick and used to be a minister. Perhaps he wanted to pray with us.

Before the day was over, our house was filled with people - my parents, who had just returned from Cancun the night before, Nick's sister Diane and her husband, my sisters and brothers-in-law, our nieces and nephews. We all surrounded his bed and prayed together.

About 4:30, the stress of the day caught up with me. I developed a terrible headache. I felt anxious, upset, emotional and out of control and decided that I needed time alone with my husband. Was that selfish? I don't know, but I felt that I deserved that time and my children deserved time alone with their daddy. I took a deep breath and asked everyone if they minded leaving for a short while. Then I would call them back. Everyone agreed and left the room.

I turned on a cassette with Twila Paris singing, "God Is In Control." A friend who knew nothing about the severity of Nick's illness had put it in our mailbox the previous October. I listened to that tape again and again. It contains other beautiful songs – "The Visitor From Heaven" and "The Everlasting Arm." With this comforting music playing in the background, I climbed into the tiny little bed with my husband. Nicholas and Lindsey joined me. This was something we'd often done as a family, and was so appropriate for the moment.

We'd always given lots of "family hugs." Nick would be standing in the kitchen and, all of a sudden, he'd run over and give me a big bear hug. Pretty soon Nicholas would join in and little Lindsey would break through all the legs to be a part of our love circle.

That day, the four of us held on to each other tightly as we lay quietly and peacefully. After we got up and left the room, I asked our son, "Nicholas, do you know what this means? Daddy is dying. Do you understand? In only a matter of time his heart will stop beating or he will stop breathing." He cried a little.

Then I explained to Lindsey what was happening. She waved the tissue in her hand back and forth, saying, "No! No!" and crawled away from me.

I said, "Lindsey, I know this is very hard. It's hard for all of us, but Daddy IS very sick and he will have to leave us."

I called everyone back in. After a final prayer as a total family, we all waited at our loved one's side.

About 9:00, our five-year-old Lindsey brought my stethoscope into her daddy's room. Remembering what I'd said earlier, she listened to his heart. She made me listen. Everybody else in the room had to listen, too. "See?" she said. "He's still breathing. His heart's still ticking."

Nicholas had quietly gone into his own room and had fallen asleep. But our little nurse never left her daddy's bedside.

She'd always been near. When I'd given him his injections, she'd hold his hand and squeeze it. She'd helped me give him his medication and held his hand while I removed his sutures. It was not out of the ordinary for her to be there in this tender time.

She even instructed the nurse, "Make sure you brush my daddy's teeth. I don't want him going to heaven with bad breath." She knew Nick always was conscientious about being clean and having clean teeth. Often he'd quoted, "Cleanliness is next to godliness."

At 10:00 the nurse returned to give Nick his medications. Thank God she was there! At 10:45 p.m., in the bedroom of our home on Jaguar Drive, Boardman, Ohio – in the home Nick loved – my beloved husband passed quietly into the eternal life. As he took his last breath, his head turned slightly and his eyes remained open. I gently closed his eyes and gazed into his face. He no longer looked like my Nick, he looked like Jesus! It seemed that a transformation had taken place.

After I phoned the funeral home, all our neighbors were called in to view him for the final time. His boss came and many of his friends. There must have been 40 people surrounding their friend and loved one.

Did Nick ever have to fear being alone? NO! If anything, he should have feared being smothered!

The hearse arrived; I opened the door and a nice young man entered. He looked around at the crowd of people and said, "Take as long as you want. Spend as much time as you want."

As the funeral car pulled away, all of our neighbors stood in their driveways, watching. I retreated into the house. I didn't want to watch Nick leave. His destination was his final resting place, his eternal home.

I prayed, "Still my head and heart, Lord. Lead me silently into the presence of your Spirit."

Our family members gathered around to support one another. We'd tried to awaken Nicholas, but he didn't want to get up. I respected that. He wanted to remember his daddy living.

Someone sent me a poem after Nick died. It's called "Safely Home."

I am home in Heaven, dear ones; Oh, so happy and bright!
There is perfect joy and beauty in the everlasting light.

All the pain and grief is over, Every restless tossing past.
I am now at peace forever, Safely home in heaven at last.

Did you wander I so calmly trod the valley of the shade?
Oh, but Jesus' love illumined every dark and fearful glade.

And He came Himself to meet me In that way so hard to tread,
And with Jesus' arm to lean on, Could I have one doubt or dread?

Then you must not grieve so sorely, For I love you dearly still:
Try to look beyond earth's shadows, Pray to trust our Father's will.

There is work still waiting for you, So you must not idly stand;
Do it now, while life remaineth – You shall rest in Jesus' land.

When that work is all completed, He will gently call you Home.
Oh, the rapture of that meeting, Oh, the joy when you come!

Farewell

The morning after my husband's body had been removed from our home, I phoned the funeral home and said, "This is Judy Shirilla, Sir. Do you have my husband there?"

"Yes," a male voice said.

I asked, "Where is he?"

"In the embalming room. ...Where else would he be?"

"Okay, I was just checking." I n order to feel safe and secure I had to know he was really there.

He's out of my hands now, I thought. *Out of my care. That's okay.*

As we begin to let go of the one we love, life becomes easier. Practice makes perfect. Gracefully let go of little things, so relinquishing major losses can be less difficult.

I've always been amazed how some people become so worldly they tightly grasp everyone and everything in their possession. Yet we go out of this world the same way we came in. When we die, we can take nothing with us except what is in our heart. What we have been and what we have done are fit legacies to leave behind.

A preacher on television once said, "Life is like a garden. We're all given the tools we need to take care of it." A bag of tools – a shovel, a hoe – and some seeds. When we begin our life, like a garden, it must be plowed. We need the sunshine in order for our plants to grow. We need the rain and the air. We also need the hardships. They prepare us for our heavenly home, so we can become precious flowers in God's garden some day.

On March 30, 1995, Nick Shirilla departed this earth to become a beautiful flower in his heavenly home. Farewell, loved one!

Nick had insisted that his children be at his funeral. I got out the list he had made of the ones he wanted for pallbearers. I was grateful we'd planned all this together several months before he died.

At one point during calling hours, I had to smile, remembering that Nick was never excited about having to wear a suit and tie for any length of time. Bob, a buddy he'd converted from being a Penn State fan to an Ohio State fan, asked me, "Judy, may I put this Ohio State hat in the coffin before they close it?"

"Sure," I told him. "Why not?" That would have pleased my husband.

Nick and his boss's wife Illene had been like sister and brother. She said, "I have a favor to ask you. Could I walk down with the pallbearers? I know this is asking a lot."

I told her, "Certainly you can. You've never asked me for anything before. Instead you've always given and given to us."

She felt honored to escort the pallbearers. Two of our brothers-in-law put the white pal over the casket. My children and I carried the offertory gifts. Illene and one of Nick's father's friends did readings.

A dear friend from our support group gave a beautiful eulogy. She began by saying, "In quietness and confidence, Nick went about his life..." That really summed it up. Nick was a quiet and gentle person, an ordinary man who had lived his life in an extraordinary way. Father then did a beautiful mass.

Some months before, Nick had said, "When I die, I hope everybody I know is there." On the day of his funeral, I looked up and said, "Nick, everybody you know is here. If they couldn't come, they sent family representatives!" The funeral director told me, "Judy, usually when you have calling hours in the afternoon, you don't have as many people come in the evening, but you had more. In fact, I had to add pages to the guest book." Not only was Nick special to me, to his children and family, he was also special to everyone who had been touched by his life.

I felt as though once again I was in the receiving line of my wedding. Just 10 short years ago I had stood in a line like this, with friends and loved ones greeting me and supporting me with their love. Only something was different this time. I was standing there alone. Yet, although Nick had gone to the other side, I felt his strength.

As we got into the funeral car, I remembered the Ohio State cap that had been placed in the casket and said to my father-in-law, "I can see Nick now – ripping off his tie and saying, 'All right! I'm glad that's over!' and putting on that Buckeye hat." We laughed together.

All Things Work For Good

Kids are resilient. The day before my husband's funeral, Nicholas and Lindsey were in the back yard playing baseball.

My dad stopped in. When he saw them, he became upset. "What are they doing, playing baseball? Their daddy just died!"

I said, "Dad, they're kids!" Within a few minutes, my

dad was out there pitching the ball. Life must go on.

Our neighbor boy, probably a freshman in high school, loved basketball. Many times Johnny had come over to talk and shoot hoops with Nick and Nicholas. The three of them had become good friends. Once he'd tried out for the basketball team, but didn't make it. Nick had said, "I really feel bad for him. He should have made it. He's good."

Two days after the funeral Nicholas asked me, "Mommy, do you know who my best friend is now?"

Remembering how often Nicholas and his dad had referred to each other as best friends, I hesitated, then asked, "No, who?"

"Johnny," my son answered.

I recalled the day Johnny had been turned down for the team and imagined that he and my husband had talked about it. Perhaps Nick might have said, "I have to go now, but if you look after Nicholas for me and make sure he plays basketball, I'll talk to God and tell Him to see that you make the team."

Johnny brought Nicholas a basketball hoop he could hang over his bedroom door and played with him often. He offered to take Nicholas to the basketball games. They have remained good friends.

Johnny told me that he had been sitting in study hall the morning Nick had died. At 10:45, the time when Nick had begun with the death rattle, Johnny had received a mental message, "Mr. Shirilla is in heaven."

I had questioned God at the time of Nick's accident. "Why did You spare him when he had the awful automobile accident, knowing he would have to endure all this suffering and chemo treatment, and was going to die from the brain tumor anyway?"

With the memories of his funeral still fresh in my mind, I realized, *Who am I to question God?* He'd said again and again, "Trust Me. Trust Me." We experienced much that was beautiful in the midst of our sadness. The beautiful funeral mass was certainly a tribute to my husband's life. Nick would never suffer again.

I finally realized, "Wow, God, now I understand Your ways are better than any!"

Nick's nurse tried to tell me, "Judy, Nick died a beautiful, peaceful death."

"How can you say that?" I asked her. "How could any death be beautiful and peaceful?"

"Trust me," she explained. "I've seen many, many cancer patients struggle with death, in and out of the hospital. You, your children and your family gave Nick a beautiful gift by keeping him in his home and loving him to the very end."

Not until a couple of years passed by did I realize the meaning of what she'd said. Nick did die a beautiful death.

Four very dear friends of mine planned a benefit dinner for us. Back in February, just before Nick had become confused, they had brought dinner to the house for Nick, the children and myself. As we all sat around the table, I remember glancing at everybody and thinking, *We must look like Jesus and His disciples at the Last Supper!* Our friends had asked my husband, "Nick would it be all right for us to have a benefit dinner dance for you?"

He smiled and shook his head up and down. "That will be fine."

They had set the date for April 2. I'd told them, "I'm not going to be at the benefit. I don't want to leave Nick's side."

God worked things out the way He always does, for the best. I was able to go to the benefit dance. Over 350 friends, family members and coworkers were there. The tribute and honor paid to my husband that evening enriched the love and support they had given us throughout my husband's illness. I am deeply thankful to many, many people.

I believe I maneuvered through my first year without my husband on automatic pilot. I took the children to a counselor to make sure they were handling their grief in a healthy way. I had energy beyond measure, attending all the children's activities. Besides playing ball, Nicholas was in Cub Scouts. I continued to enroll Lindsey in dance lessons. She learned to twirl the baton and loved it.

I used to tell Nick, "Don't you dare make a tomboy out of my little girl!" When she turned seven, she wanted to play softball, so I signed her up. Obviously, she'd inherited that Shirilla athletic ability and I inherited my husband's enthusiasm for sports. I was at every practice for both children. That had been Nick's "thing" while he was alive while I did the cooking and cleaning up. I began to experience a new relationship with my children I'd never shared with them before.

Many months earlier, I'd watched a video about cancer. The woman who narrated told about a gentleman who had gone through a lot of tragedy. When he could no longer work in his normal capacity, he became a good painter. She concluded, "When God closes a door, He opens a window." I believe that. New relationships with new meanings form. My relationship with my children became my new window.

During Nick's illness I'd jokingly asked, "God, you've closed so many doors. Where is that window, because I'd like to jump out!" Many times I felt I wanted to run away, but where would I go?

Once again I'd looked for that window and had found it in my children's activities. I thought, "Here we are – Judy, Nicholas and Lindsey. But the biggest part of all you've had is gone." The empty chair every day at the dinner table, the empty chair in the living room, the loneliness was very different for me. I had never been alone.

When I was growing up, I had shared my room with my sister. Then I got married and shared my room with Nick. After 35 years of life I had my own room for the first time. I didn't like it. Being alone took some getting used to.

In the book of Romans God promised that all things work for good to those who trust Him and live according to His plan. In spite of our pain and grief, many parts of our life were working out for good.

X.
MY JOB CHANGE AND FURTHER LOSS

The Aftermath

Three months after Nick's funeral, I made the difficult decision to return to work. I didn't realize how filled my schedule had been. Finally exhaustion set in. How long can your body function in this fight or flight mode? For eight years I had been in the fight mode.

One day after I returned home from work, I lay back on the swing on my deck, looking up at the sky. Suddenly I felt as though God had lifted a building off my shoulders. I told Him, "God, thank you. You will take better care of Nick than I ever could."

I continued to work the 3:00 to 11:00 shift for one year. The first Thanksgiving without Nick, the children had to spend the night at my parents' because I had to go to work. I told my mom, "I feel so bad that I have to leave my children and go to work on a holiday. They don't have their daddy, and now their mommy can't be with them."

Of course, they were with their grandparents, and all their cousins were there for the day, so it didn't bother them nearly as much as it bothered me. I told one of my coworkers, "I have to look for a new job. This is the last holiday I'm going to work."

I began to ask God for a change in employment. Often I talked things over with my husband as if he were here. I told him, "Nick, you know how much I used to complain about this job. Please tell God to help me find a new one."

In May of 1996, I applied at a new outpatient surgery center in our area. Although there were over 500 applicants, I was chosen for an interview and was hired to work part time in pre-op and recovery. I was ecstatic!

I quit the hospital and went to work in a beautiful brand new facility equipped with the latest technology. It was a job any nurse would dream about – daytime hours, good salary, no weekends or holidays and only five minutes away from our home.

My first day on the job, something miraculous occurred. My grief, my deep, deep sadness lifted. Life seemed wonderful once again. I think it was because I had spent 11 years working in a hospital setting, plus many days and nights in hospitals with Nick. A hospital is a hospital. Leaving that type of setting and entering new surroundings became an important part of my healing process. I looked forward to my new job – the challenge and the opportunity.

Les Brown, a motivational speaker, is a source of inspiration to me. I had listened to his tapes frequently. He talks about the power to change, about being positive and surviving difficult situations. I'd often thought about his questions, "Are you staying in a job that's making you miserable? Don't you wish some day you could drive there and keep on driving by?" Then he'd laugh. "Is your job making you sick? Why don't you leave?"

He added, "People will stay in the most miserable situation – known horrors – because they don't want to take that first step out the door to freedom." I had taken that step and was excited.

At first I loved my work, my coworkers, the facility – everything about my new job. But suddenly that evil messenger returned. Do you know about Murphy's Law? If anything can go wrong, it will.

It wasn't long until another bubble burst. This time it was pricked in the workplace by politics, scrutiny, jealousy and malicious acts to bring me down deliberately. At first I tried to avoid what was happening and go with the flow.

One gal commented, "You're willing to do anything!" I always had been willing to do whatever was asked of me.

I told her, "That's right. I like it here. I appreciate my job, it's so different from working in a hospital. The hours are better, the patients do well."

Patients wrote compliments about me on their evaluations. Several times the doctor told me, "You're doing a good job."

I tried to solve the problem and maintain my focus by transferring to another department. The more I tried to stay on top, the more I was pulled down. It didn't take me long to learn there was very little organization, the standards of care were low, a lot of people wanted to be in charge without shouldering the accompanying responsibility. They pushed their jobs off on the rest of us. Evidently the staff did not value good, conscientious nurses. Patient care had become a business.

I could not compromise my nursing license that I'd worked so hard for. And I certainly could not compromise the quality of patient care.

Finally I realized that light and darkness do not mix. Somebody had to leave. Guess who? Me. In January 1997, I resigned, a decision which was not easy for me to make, even though I knew I was doing the right thing. To date, 15 nurses, coworkers and secretaries have been forced to do the same thing.

To my surprise, I re-experienced the grief process – shock, denial and anger. *Why did I have to leave? I liked it there. Why didn't the miserable people have to leave?* I became depressed and began to grieve the loss of my husband more intensely than before.

I was ready to take my resume to another facility immediately. But my dad, although he was a strong advocate of the work ethic, advised, "Judy, take some time off. You went through a lot of stress during Nick's illness and you've been through so much stress on that job. Take some time off and spend it with your children."

I sensed God was talking to me through my earthly father and I'd better listen. I took the remainder of the winter and that summer off. It was the best summer of my life. We bought a beautiful oval swimming pool. The children and I spent much quality time together, which helped me unravel much of my stress. We managed to laugh again.

Then came June. I was suffering blurred vision and insisting it was from stress. The doctor agreed, "It could be stress." I wondered if my eyes had been damaged from all the radiation my husband received.

I defended my case. "I had a lot of visual grief with my husband. I saw him seize a lot."

He said, "Let me take a closer look." He diagnosed a hereditary eye disease called StarGardt's, a juvenile form of macular degeneration.

This couldn't be happening! I'd suffered the worst losses of my life – first my husband, then the loss of my job - and now my eyesight was going! I tried to joke about it. "What could be worse than being 35, a widow, and now I'm going blind!" But it wasn't funny.

Eyesight is so precious. Too often we take it for granted.

When I returned to the doctor, he assured me, "If you have this condition at all, it's a mild form.

In September, when I went to get my driver's license renewed, my eye condition brought another challenge. I could not pass the exam to get my night time driver's license. I was devastated! I went to five different license bureaus and each time I was turned down. I argued to myself, "They're nuts! Their machine must be broken. Something isn't right, I see fine!"

As my sister and I were driving down the road, we spotted a sign in front of a Christian church that said, "Problems are not problems. They are messages from God." I believe God was giving me a message, trying to slow me down. I had kept up a phenomenal pace for years, constantly on the run. Now He was saying through my eye problem, "Quit driving. Stay home and rest." And I did.

In the months that followed I purchased a lot of vita-min therapy; got plenty of rest, relaxation, exercise, and healthy eating – a lot of greens. My choices have helped minimize the progression of my eye condition. I am even driving again at night. Life does get better.

XI.
EPILOGUE

A Mended Peanut

Recently, I was having "one of those days." My neighbor had just been diagnosed with cancer. Only 50 years old! I felt bad. I pulled into the gas station and jumped out of my van to pump the gas, but the nozzle had a bag over it, and a sign that said, "Out of order."

I thought, *Gee! That's the kind of day I'm having! Out of order!*

I jumped back into the van and pulled over to another pump. As I waited for the customer ahead of me to get done, I thought, *Wait a minute! ...Out of order? That's a great title for the book I've been wanting to write. Out of order! Everything that's happened in my life from the day Nick and I purchased our home has been out of order.*

At an early age I became a widow. Out of order! At an early age I was forced into retirement from my nursing career. Out of order! At an early age I was told my vision was impaired due to a hereditary disease. Out of order! These things aren't supposed to happen until a person is far more advanced in the aging process. I was convinced that "Out of Order" was the right title for my book, but I had to add a subtitle. "Faith is Strengthened, Hope Blossoms, and Love Conquers After Loss."

If your life has been knocked out of order, I hope you will appreciate the story our Pastor recently told in his homily. He asked, "Have you ever felt like a peanut that's been dropped in Yankee Stadium and everybody is tramping on you?" He concluded by saying, "Don't despair. Have hope.

God isn't finished with us yet."

My imagination ran away with me. I could see this shiny, silvery elephant entering Yankee Stadium and walking out on the baseball field. Everybody is watching him and cheering. The game had to be put on hold.

The elephant roams around the field. What do you think he's looking for? He's hungry, so he's looking for fallen peanuts. All of a sudden, at the very far edge of the field, he stops because he spies a broken, crushed peanut – one that's been stepped on many times.

That big elephant tips his head and looks at that poor little smashed peanut. He lets down his trunk, then says to himself, "Something is different about this peanut. I can't eat this poor smashed peanut!"

The little peanut looks up and says in a pitiful voice, "Can you help me?"

The elephant says, "Yes, I think I can." With a tear of compassion in his eye, he gently nuzzles the peanut with his trunk until all its broken pieces are back in place.

The little peanut looks up again, with half a smile on its face, and says, "Hey, this is great! Did you do this all by yourself?"

The elephant says, "No, I had a lot of help from God."

"Then thanks to both of you."

Suddenly the elephant lifts that peanut up and lovingly begins to carry her so high that she can never get stepped on again.

Maybe you've been crushed many times in life, by the loss of a loved one, the loss of your job or a health problem. Remember, no matter how out of order our lives may become, if we continue to have faith, hope, and love, we, too, can conquer anything.

"Now abide faith, hope, love, these three; but the greatest of these is love." I Corinthians 13:13

REFERENCES

Brown, Les. Courage To Live Your Dreams. Sound recording (6 cassettes). New York: Harper Audio, 1993.

Carlton Collection Cards, Toronto, Ontario MAZ 1S7, AGC, Inc., 1999.

"Footprints." (author unknown)

Johnson, Barbara. Pain Is Inevitable But Misery Is Optional. So, Stick A Geranium In Your Hat And Be Happy! Dallas: Word Publications, 1990.

Kushner, Harold S. When Bad Things Happen To Good People. Schockner Books, 2nd ed. New York, 1989.

"Love is Patient." New American Bible, First Letter Paul to Corinthians, Ch 13.

Matthews, Emily. Believe In Miracles.

Paris, T. and Brown, B. Beyond Dream. Sound recording, 1994.

"Safely Home." (author unknown).

Schuller, Robert H. Tough Times Never Last But Tough People Do. Sound recording. Chicago, IL: Nightingale-Conant Corporation, 1984.

The Vindicator. "What Cancer Cannot Do," 1992.